A MENNONITE OF KISERU

A MENNONITE OF KISERU

An Autobiography as told to Joseph C. Shenk

Eastern Mennonite Board of Missions and Charities
Salunga, Pennsylvania 17538
1984

I dedicate this book to the memory of my father, Kisare, son of Mbayee, through whose life I came into the world and whose specific love for me gave me a sound basis on which I could grow into a knowledge of God my Creator, Savior, and Lord.

—*Z. Marwa Kisare*

Contents

Acknowledgments

My gratitude is to Eastern Mennonite Board of Missions and Charities, Salunga, Pennsylvania, who have agreed that my autobiography be written. They have provided the considerable financial and administrative resources which have made this possible.

I am grateful to Joseph C. Shenk, a son in Christ, who has given of himself to translate my Swahili into English. I have put myself into his hands, trusting him to record faithfully the intent of the words of my story. In telling my history I have not spoken disrespectfully toward any person whose life has intersected with mine. Any dishonor or disrespect which may be read into the story is an inaccurate reflection of my narration.

Praise be to the God and Father of our Lord Jesus Christ who has given me, a herdsman of Kiseru, the opportunity to give honor to him, even to those who are much greater than I.

—*Z. Marwa Kisare*
Shirati, August 1983

I am indebted to Omar E. Eby, who gave editorial guidance as the manuscript was prepared for publication.

—*Joseph C. Shenk*

Preface

Mennonites, tradition tells us, are from Switzerland, South Germany, Holland, the Ukraine, Alberta, Pennsylvania, the Chaco.... But here is the story of a Mennonite from Kiseru on the eastern shores of Lake Victoria in Tanzania, East Africa. What sort of Kiseru man is he who would call himself "Mennonite"? Here is his portrait, the story of a black Anabaptist.

Kisare's story is a missionary story. But it is different, different because it's Kisare's story. The traditional missionary story tells of those who went to distant lands carrying the gospel message. Kisare is the flip side of that traditional story. He tells us here about receiving the gospel.

Faith is dynamic in Africa, a vital part of everyone's daily experience. In the urban Western experience models no longer exist through which to relate to the biblical narrative. But Africa is still rich in traditions which closely parallel the Old Testament culture, faith, economy. So the flip side of Kisare's receiving the gospel is that as he makes that gospel his own, and tells us about it, he becomes a missionary to us, completing the circle of witness, so to speak.

I began to know Bishop Kisare well in 1970 when I became his companion and driver, taking him in his LandRover everywhere he went over a period of about 18 months. Talking with him, listening in on the conversation in the LandRover when I was usually the only white present, and listening to his sermons during a score of weekend spiritual life conferences, I became convinced that he should sometime tell his story to a larger audience.

A couple of years ago I approached representatives of Eastern Mennonite Board of Missions, Salunga, Pennsylvania, with the proposal that they make it possible for me to

spend some time with Bishop Kisare so that I might help
him write his story. They agreed to this. I became a guest of
the Kisares at Shirati, Tanzania, in 1983, for three months,
mid-May to mid-August.

Every morning the Bishop gave me two hours in his
home, a fresh tablecloth spread on the dining-room table, the
appropriate passage from *Daily Light* read and commented
on, prayer for each other and for the day's work, followed by
the Bishop's reflections on his life. Daily at 10:30 a.m. we
were served sweet milk-tea or millet gruel. As the manuscript
took shape, we spent time reading it together.

From time to time I was the Kisares' guest for a meal.
Once he slaughtered a ram for me, occasionally a chicken. I
accompanied the Bishop and Mama seven times on weekend
visits, a number of them overnight, to the rural areas, partici-
pating in a wedding, baptism and communion services, a
church dedication and three youth rallies. I was happy once
again to serve in the capacity of driver.

During my three months at Shirati, I accompanied the
Bishop and Mama as guest to numerous African homes,
where we were plied repeatedly with beef, chicken, mutton,
goat, *uchuri* (a sauce made from a goat's intestinal juices),
and fish, as seasoning for *ugali* (African bread), rice, and
sweet potatoes. I drank more cups of tea and yogurt and
more calabashes of millet gruel than I care to count.

Bishop Kisare and I have tried to reflect with integrity
the story of a community in rapid social change struggling to
form a viable synthesis between its traditional roots and the
reality of being part of the modern world family of peoples.
We have seen the church as the reality around which this
change is taking place. It is our hope that in this story
nothing of disparagement or unkindness has been said of
anyone, that in this, our summer's work, the person and
work of our Lord Jesus Christ be glorified.

—Joseph C. Shenk

Fish traps, otulo *in the Luo language*

Two sons of Kisare and Okech: Marwa, with glasses, is conversing with his older brother, Otulo.

Childhood

Kiseru, My Country

My mother, Okech, told me how it was when I was born. When she was a new bride to my father, Kisare, she had no trouble getting pregnant. That wasn't her problem. The problem was that each child died soon after it was born. The years passed and children were birthed, but none lived. Then one year a son was born and the other women in the village said to my mother, "Okech, throw your son out."

They told her, "Maybe there is one who sees into your heart and knows how much you want a child, how you long for a son. Maybe this one is pleased to see you pained. This one is joyful to see your yearly anguish as you celebrate birth and death together. Trick this one whose eye is on that which you bear. Toss your newborn son into the thicket. Throw him out with the afterbirth and thus show that your heart is not knit to this your offspring."

Mother thought about this advice. There was a certain logic to it. So she threw her son into the weeds beyond the village enclosure. But she didn't throw him naked and unprotected. Mother secured him in a reed fish trap, fastening him safely so no passing animal might molest him. Shortly after this new boy had been "thrown out," a young daughter of the village "happened" to pass that way. She heard a baby's cry and "found" a newborn boy in a fish trap, there in the thicket. He was alive, yelling lustily, arms and legs pushing, kicking against the confines of his tiny cage.

"I've found a child, a man child," she called out. "I found him in a fish trap by the path. See, he's newborn. Life is in him."

13

The villagers gathered around. "What is to be done with this child?" they asked one another.

"Give the boy to Okech," Father decreed. "She has recently given birth and her breasts are full of milk. She has no child. Let her suckle this one. Let his name be Otulo—fish trap—in memory of how he was found."

Otulo lived. He is my older brother.

In the rhythm of time, Okech again became pregnant, again she gave birth, again a son. This time Father intervened. He told mother, "Quit this women's foolishness of throwing babies in the bushes." But the fear from all those other deaths was still in my mother. She pleaded with Father to do something, to take some step to protect this boy too.

Father called a doctor. I was small, newborn, unknowing. The doctor picked me up from my mother's arms, laughing at my tight-eyed wincing from the bright clear light of day there away from the shade of the thatched house where Mother sat. The doctor put a pinch of medicine to my nose making me sneeze again and again.

"Life is in this one," the doctor said. "This son of the earth will live."

Father named me Marwa because that was the doctor's name, but he affectionately nicknamed me Woud Kondo—Son of a Feathered Headdress—because of the ostrich plumes the day I first sneezed, so many ostrich feathers, black and white, waving gaily from the doctor's headdress.

After me, Mother bore two more sons. They both lived. My two younger brothers were given names in the normal way because by then Mother had forgotten those years when all her babies died.

When I was about two years old, a war began in Europe. That was 1914. It was a war between the Germans and the British. Our home was in Tanganyika, German East Africa. We lived just a few miles south of the Tanganyika border with Kenya, which was a British colony. Soon the war spread to where we lived. The Germans taxed us, taking our cattle to feed their Tanganyika army.

My father was not a joiner. He was a loner, independent. He kept out of other people's quarrels. No German was going to take his cattle to feed a white man's army. So Father went north, crossing the border into Kenya with his wives and children and his large herds of cattle, sheep, and goats. He was a wealthy man.

African chiefs appointed by the Germans and loyal to them reported my father's move. They told them, "Kisare, son of Mbayee, has fled to Kenya, but he has not yet crossed the Kuja River."

German officers sent soldiers after him into Kenya. Father was unable to protect himself because he was south of the river. The soldiers took all of Father's cattle except for those cows which had recently given birth and couldn't travel quickly. We lived there in Kenya just north of the border until the white man's war was over. The border itself was a white man's boundary, a line that ran right through Girango country. My father was Girango.

Very long ago a herdsman named Girango moved with his family out of the Nile River Valley. He traveled south and east with his wives and children, flocks and herds. He settled to the north-east of the great Lake Nam, the lake which we know today as Victoria. Girango was a Nilotic. There are many Nilotic peoples. Girango was of the Luo people. Yet the name "Girango" means "Bantu." I think that this first Luo person who moved into the country that is now the South Nyanza Province of Kenya quickly adopted certain Bantu customs and ways of life. This made him compatible with the Suba people who were living here first. The Suba are a Bantu people. We might think of Girango as a Luo who was somewhat Bantuized by his new neighbors.

In any case, the Girango-Luo are shorter and browner than their Nilotic cousins in Northern Uganda and Southern Sudan. Some of the Girango names have Bantu roots, and many of them use a Bantu dialect in addition to the dominant Luo language.

Girango's sons who came with him out of the Nile River Valley were Geta, Gire, Kisero, and Tegi. These men became heads of clans. The areas where they lived took their names. Although the Girango clans had distant destinations in mind, they migrated only a few miles at a time, thus giving opportunity for acculturation and assimilation so they would not antagonize the Suba inhabitants of the land.

Kisero with his family moved by stages farther southward, settling finally in the area where I was born just south of what later came to be the border between Kenya and Tanganyika.

The patriarch Kisero bore two sons, Kisero and Kine, and one daughter, Rieri. The families of these three children populated the areas which became known as Kiseru, Kine, and Burieri. Of the three clans, Kisero was the strongest. Today on modern maps the name Kiseru is given to the territory surrounding Shirati.

Kisero himself had two sons, Kamang'indi and Kamsangia. So there are two families in the Kisero clan. People do not intermarry within either family. My father, Kisare, son of Mbayee, was from the Kamang'indi family of the Kisero clan of the Girango people. Girango was our ancestor who came from the north.

During the past century other Luo people migrated out of the Nile River Valley into the area northwest of Lake Victoria. They haven't taken on Bantu ways. These more recent arrivals from the north are thought of as the pure Luo people. My mother, Okech, was a pure Luo.

When the war was over, Father decided to move back to Tanganyika. Before the war we lived in Kiseru country but my father, ever the loner, settled north of Kiseru this time, in the Burieri country at a place called Kirongwe. That was just a mile from the Kenya border.

The close of the war brought another change. The English took the place of the Germans as our colonial masters. Tanganyika became a trust territory under the new League of Nations. The British were assigned by the League of Nations to administer the country.

The Village, My Boyhood Home

Every several years my father would marry a young wife who would revitalize his village. Okech, my mother, was Sixth Wife. I remember that Father's had from 12 to 15 wives. He died when I was 12. A boy that age isn't concerned with the number of his mothers, so I'm not exactly sure how many wives he had. I remember only that there were many mothers, older ones and younger ones. Sons of First Wife were already married and had children by the time I was born. I was one of the younger sons of my father.

Our village, as with all Luo villages, was in the shape of a big circle. The houses were round and they were placed in a circle, also round—everything "O." A fence built of logs (tree trunks and branches) stood on end, dug into the earth, log against log, connected house to house. So there was a protected area, the area "inside the village" which was separated from the outside by the barrier of houses and fence or wall.

There was one gap, or doorway, in the fence. This was the entrance to our village. The doorway was an open space framed by tree trunks placed in a big A. The space was just wide enough for a cow's horns to pass, low enough that a grown man needed to stoop. At night logs were piled across the entrance, making the village secure against wild animals and thieves.

The village circle was big with room for new houses as they were needed. All the houses were around the edge of the circle interlocked by the village fence. Each wife had her own house. Small children slept in their mother's house, but when they were no longer children they slept in youth houses built for them. Father also had his personal house.

Each house was placed in the circle according to the status of the person who lived in it. First Wife's house was directly opposite the village entrance. Father's house was to the left of the village entrance some distance from First Wife's house. His two youngest wives had their houses next to his, one on the right and one on the left. Father's care was the main responsibility of his youngest wives, so their houses were close to his. The older wives' houses were ranked next to First Wife's house according to their position in the family. The youth houses were at the entrance to the village.

Father's mother died long before I was born. In a Luo village the patriarch's widowed mother, or mothers, each have a house built in the line of houses around the village circle. The grandmother's work in the village is to be the teacher of the teenage girls. These older girls sleep in Grandmother's house and this becomes a "school" for them to learn how a woman should act in our society. Grandmother teaches them about men and babies, firewood and cooking, work and play, and about right and wrong.

In Father's village there was no grandmother so the youths of the village, both boys and girls, slept in the houses at the entrance to the village. Father knew everything that happened in his village. Father was stern but he was also just. His wives and children were afraid of his discipline. This fear protected us from doing anything wrong there in our village where I lived as a boy.

Each house in the village was round with a conical grassroof. The outer wall was of logs, upended, dug into the earth, tied together with plant fibers and chinked with mud, not just any mud but a special formula of various soils. The inside plaster, smoothed on with a woman's hand, contained cow manure, giving a hard, non-cracking finish.

Each house had two doors. One public door opened on to the center of the village. The other private door opened to the outside of the village. Each house had two rooms. A straight wall of sturdy sticks separated the private sleeping and cooking third of the house from the larger public room. The woman's cooking fire was in the private part of the house at the foot of her bed. Her water pot and grinding stone were in the corner near the fire.

Every wife had a granary outside her house. The granary was a large round basket woven of reeds and plastered inside. It was seven feet high and five feet across. The granary stood on a base of crossed logs raising it off the ground. For a lid, the granary had a round roof thatched with grass. A small ladder was at the side of the granary. You could open this big basket by tipping the roof up on one side with a long pole.

The cattle corral was in the middle of the village enclosure. It was built of larger tree trunks and logs than those used for the fence that went around the outer circle of the village linking the houses. The corral was a fortress within a fortress. Cattle was our wealth. Father was careful to protect his wealth from wild animals and thieves.

Father's many animals—cattle, goats, and sheep—were

divided up and assigned around the village. That way each mother and her children were responsible for certain specific animals. At night the cows, bulls and oxen were all herded into the corral. But the goats, sheep and small calves slept in the house of the woman who was responsible for them. The animals slept in the larger, public side of the house. Every morning the first task in a home was to chase out the goats and sheep and sweep the house clean.

My mother hadn't many animals to care for because she never bore a daughter. When a daughter is married, her father receives cattle and goats and sheep from her husband's family. This bride wealth seals the marriage covenant. Whenever one of my half sisters was married, Father would keep some of the animals for his personal use, but most of them would be assigned to the girl's mother. Some of my older mothers had daughters who were getting married. So these mothers had many goats and sheep, and they had many cows to milk. But my own mother, having only sons, was poor.

In the early morning Father would pull away the logs sealing the entrance to the corral. The cows would go from the corral to the house where the calves slept. The cows were milked in the house. Father always kept from 18 to 24 cows for his personal use. From the time I was about nine years old, Father assigned me to milk his cows. Father's children never went near his house except for a special reason. To me it seemed a great honor, like being invited to State House today, to be assigned the work of milking his cows.

I would get up very early, before it was yet light, and go to his house. The cows would come, each in her turn, into the larger public side of Father's house. The calf would suckle a bit; then I would tie it near the cow's head to a post along the wall of the house. Then I would squat beside the cow and stroke long pulls of creamy milk from her udder into my calabash. Each cow gave only a quart or so. It didn't take too long to milk them all.

As I said, it was the responsibility of Father's two youngest wives to care for him. Their houses were next to his house, one on the right and one on the left along the O of the village. The older wives who had the children to care for, had less responsibility for Father.

When I went to milk his cows, Father would instruct his youngest and most loved wife to be sure I had breakfast before returning to Mother's house. She would be on the other side of the partition where the bed was, rhythmically churning yogurt, separating curds from whey in her long narrow gourd. From the darkness near the smoky, early-lit fire came the sounds of "swoosh ka-sluush, swoosh ka-sluush," its rhythm syncopated with the "shust-shust, shust-shust," of milk pumped by my little fists squirting into the calabash held tightly between my knees. One by one I filled calabashes and various pots, setting them here and there—my morning's harvest of food from Father's cows.

> I am in my father's house at break of day with the sounds and smells of caring all around telling me, "You are warm and loved; your father opens his door to you and makes your welfare the concern of his most loved and youngest wife."

Kisare, My Father

Father had many sons, and by the time I was born he had grandsons too. He paid little attention to his individual children. The only way Father would take special interest in any one of his many sons was if he should see something special in one of them. Then he might love that son.

In Father's old age he singled me out for special love and attention. He must have liked what he saw in me. He never told me directly why he loved me. I think it was because he saw no pretense or sham in me, no ingratiation. I was just me, Marwa, black, chunky lad, milk-fattened cheeks, sober-eyed and solemn about my duties. Father liked my work. He noted especially the straightforward way in which I herded goats. Whenever I think about my childhood and my relationship to Father, it is goatherding that stands out.

Goats were the responsibility of the village's pre-pubescent boys. Most of the area around Kirongwe was savannah. Free-standing trees and thickets were scattered about over the grasslands. It was hilly country, granite outcroppings here and there. The streams flowed when it rained and dried up during the dry season. The low places along the water courses were full of acacia and fig trees growing up through a tangle of thorn scrub.

Some of the land was farmed, maybe 2 percent of it. Our little millet farms were dug by hand, unfenced. The goatherd's job was to keep his goats from getting into any of the cultivated plots. He also had to keep them clear of any thickets where a leopard might lurk. It was important to the goatherd not to lose any goats, to come home in the evening with the same number he started out with in the morning. Goatherding is a difficult job because goats are never still. They are always going off in all directions. Boys aged six to ten are also easily distracted and can quickly forget to keep an eye on the goats.

Goatherding in our village was an elaborate business. From six to ten boys worked together. In the morning when the goats had been driven well clear of the village, the oldest of the boys in the group of herders would take up a position on a bit of high ground, an anthill or rock. From his vantage point he could see what was going on on all sides. He was the boss and he would tell the little boys what to do.

When I became old enough to take my turn at being chief goatherd, I was too curious about the savannah to stay perched on an anthill all day yelling instructions to my younger brothers. I found that if I kept ahead of the lead goat, I could influence somewhat where he went and the rest generally followed. So on my days in charge we would roam far and wide across the savannah.

As we roamed, we would often chase up quail and other seed-eating birds. I had my throwing sticks with me and many times I would bring home in the evening dove, quail, francolin. Soon it became wasteful for all the boys to come along because I could easily manage the herd with only two helpers. So the technique of goatherding changed in our village, and only a few boys went out on the savannah each day with the goats.

It was a grave irresponsibility for a goatherd to let the goats stray into a cultivated field. Goats can quickly devastate a budding millet crop. When goats get into a field, the owner of the field has the right to beat the goatherd mercilessly. Only once in my years of herding Father's goats was I so careless that they got into a millet field.

The owner of the field saw what had happened. But he didn't shout to wake me from my careless daydreaming. Instead, he sneaked up on me and springing out from behind some bushes, he grabbed me suddenly before I could dart away. He struck me only twice with his stick. People were afraid to harm a child of Kisare because Father was a rich and powerful man, so the man struck me "one, two" and ceased. He didn't tell Father. I didn't tell Father either. So no one knew until after I was married that I had been careless one day and my goats had strayed into a millet field.

When I was herding, I would work the goats around during the day so that by midafternoon I would be back not too far from Father's village. Father would come looking for us, followed on the path by the woman he loved, his youngest wife. When he would come to the area where he expected to find us, he would call, "Wuod Kondo, bi—Son of a Feathered Headdress—come." Usually I would hear him right away. I would go with my two helpers to where he was. Youngest Mother would give us the food she had brought with her.

While we boys squatted around the pot of food, Father would go off to watch the goats. Usually our meal was a lentil paste bathed in a pool of clear, golden ghee, a rarefied butter extracted from milk curds. I reached, two-fingered, down through the ghee for a scoop of greens to lift dripping to my lips. Only men with many cattle could have their food prepared in ghee. I remember still its rich aroma—the food of a wealthy man.

When we were finished eating, Youngest Mother would take the pot and return home, but Father often lingered on the savannah coming home with us in the evening.

I didn't herd goats every day. Other brothers my age took turns with me.

During those happy boyhood years my greatest joy was hunting for the aluru—Harlequin quail. They are fat little fellows which run hidden through the grasses. You can often hear the black-and-white-throated male whistling for his mate, a four noted "pleet, pleet—pleet, pleet." They migrate with the rains. Large numbers of them would appear on the savannah as our millet fields were ripening in April and May.

They would hide in the grasses and were quiet whenever anyone came near to where they were. Then when you were almost on top of them they would startle you by bursting out of the grass with a loud whirr of wings.

My weapon was the *rungu*—knobkerrie. By trial and error I found that for my weapon to fly true the knob had to be small and somewhat flat, the stick long, from 2½ to three feet. Other boys, would-be hunters, searched the bushes for a large knot or a place where several branches came out of the main stem. Sometimes they would dig out the root mass of a bush and from it carefully shape a big round ball the size of an orange with one sturdy stem protruding for a handle. "A beautiful *rungu*," these boys would boast, "so large a head, so smooth and round!" But their polished clubs pitched end over end when thrown and never hit anything.

My knobkerries had balance. They would spin like pinwheels about their centers. I would carry a whole handful of special hunting sticks, four or five of them. When hunting, it is important not to become startled. You must keep your cool when the *aluru* bursts on a whirr of wings out of the grass at your feet. The quail's intent is to make you jump in surprise. Before you recover he will be far out of range of your *rungu.*

When I would flush a covey into the air, I would wait just a moment giving them time to stabilize their flight, to establish a trajectory. Then I would focus on just one bird and throw my *rungu* spinning after it. I seldom missed; I was really devastating. Smaller boys would hunt with me, gathering up the fallen quail one by one to take home to their mothers. Toward evening I would keep some for myself, taking them back to the village for Father or Mother.

I remember a day when I was seven or eight. It was near the end of the yearly food cycle and I went hunting. Afternoon thunderheads were building up, the marshy valleys soggy from yesterday's cloudburst. I had five knobkerries and five times I threw bringing down five quail.

I am now standing in my father's house. He sees my shining eyes, my shy smile held tight over milk-white teeth. I am holding in front of me, high so he can see, a clutch of plump *aluru* hanging upside down, little quail feet held tightly in my trembling hands. Father is pleased. He chuckles beneath his breath from there where he sits near the back wall beyond the beer pot; his bright eyes smile at me out of the dim recess of the room. "*Woud Kondo*," he says, "my little Son of the Ostrich Plumes, you are good. Your knobkerrie once thrown never falls until it falls together with its prey. Ahh, yes, my *Woud Kondo*."

Father called Youngest Mother, who came quickly to take my offering. She smoked the meat over a low fire for several days and then cooked it with ghee, producing a succulent sauce for the evening *ugali* meal. I still remember the taste and aroma of that tender meat prepared for Father and me by his youngest wife.

Beer, a home brew, has always had an important place in our society. But Father, loner that he was, would not participate in community drinking parties. On special occasions, maybe to celebrate the harvest, he would call two or three close friends, men his age, and they would have a party. They would sit in his house, reclined against the semicircle of the house's outer wall, in their midst the beer pot, a yeasty millet blend. Each man had a drinking straw made from a hollowed reed. Father's straw was about five feet long but some of his friends had straws seven or more feet long. These drinking reeds were carried from place to place in a piece of hollow bamboo to protect their fragile length. The length of the straws allowed the men to sit comfortably around the room with everyone drinking from the common pot.

It was customary at large beer parties for the host to invite young women from the surrounding villages to come and sing his praises. The women would form a circle and dance—two steps forward, one back, rhythmic foot beats syncopated with clap of hand and swaying body. As they danced, they sang songs praising their host. But Father considered such dances foolish. He was suspicious of vain displays of wealth and influence. Our neighbors, knowing Father's disdain for their noisy parties, never invited him to the big beer bashes.

I never saw Father perform any act of worship. It may be that he worshiped, but I was not aware of his doing so. I was only about 12 when he died and I wasn't very aware of religious things. The most common religious ceremony when I was a boy was for the father of a village to ask an itinerant shaman or diviner to come and put the village right. This religious activity was called *kutengeneza mji*—to straighten up the village. The father of a village was always concerned that no spirit or power would disrupt the harmony of the village, causing illness or death among the people or cattle. The shaman was invited to come and *tengeneza mji* even when everything was going well. Such a visit could be thought of as routine preventative maintenance.

When the shaman came to straighten up the village, he would poke around here and there and ask questions. Then he would usually prescribe a blood sacrifice to honor the spirit of a departed ancestor. Often the sacrifice would be of a rooster of solid color—black, white, red—killed over the ancestor's grave, allowing the blood squirting from the neck stump to sprinkle the grave. Only the ancestors who had died recently, going back no more than two or three generations, were honored in this way.

By doing this sacrifice the shaman was putting everything into proper covenant relationship between the ancestors and the living members of the village. The shaman would also recommend various charms to protect the people or cattle from various ills caused by Satan or evil spirits. Some of these charms were worn by people to protect them from bad luck or illness. Other charms were to be hung at the entrance to the village or at the entrance to a house.

If something had already gone wrong in a village, the shaman would be called. This visit was more serious than a maintenance visit because a satan or evil spirit had already entered the village. The shaman now needed to drive the evil thing out of the village.

Sometimes when something went wrong in a village, it was caused by an ancestor as a punishment on someone or on the village as a whole for something wrong that was done. The shaman had to divine the reason for the problem. Then he would prescribe the correct sacrifice to put things right again. If the problem was caused by a broken covenant between the village and an ancestor, then a spotless white sheep had to be sacrificed to make the village well again. A goat was never used for a sacrifice.

The sacrificial sheep's blood was mixed with the

digested grasses from the sheep's small intestine and with other herbal medicines that the shaman had brought with him. This mixture was sprinkled over the ancestor's grave and in various places in the village. Sometimes it was sprinkled on the people in the village, depending on the nature of the problem. In the end the shaman would take a mouthful and spew it out at the sun, praying, "Look well on this village."

These religious ceremonies were common when I was a boy. But my father, Kisare, would have nothing to do with shamans. None of his wives or children wore charms prescribed by them. Only after Father's death were religious ceremonies done in our village. My oldest living half-brother became responsible for the village when Father died. He was the second son of Father's First Wife. By the time Father died this brother already had three wives and many children. At his mother's urging he asked the shamans to come to our village. To me this practice was strange, a change from Father's ways.

I remember Father as a man given to anger, a man whose word was law in his village. He wore a bell on a leather thong around his right leg just below the knee. It was oblong, a piece of metal beaten round forming a hollow with a metal ball inside. The bell was fastened on the outside of his leg and as he walked the ball was jarred about in its little cylinder, ringing "ching-chingili, ching-chingili, ching-chingili." My older brothers and sisters, who lived in the houses at the village entrance were terrified of him. Whenever they heard him approaching, they would keep well under cover until he had passed.

Looking back across the years, I think now that Father was timid and insecure. Seeing him now through the lens of my own experience, I see that his shouting was just his blustering way of hiding a timid spirit.

Okech, My Mother

Large polygamous villages were really a collection of households. Each wife was responsible for her own children. The husband, or village head, was a little like God in the Luo world view of God. He was distant from and uninvolved with the daily affairs of each household. If there was a major crisis, then the village head would look into the matter. Or if one of his sons was taking a wife or one of his daughters was being married, then he would be involved in the necessary arrangements. But on a day-to-day basis each wife was responsible for her own children and ran the affairs of her own household.

There was a hierarchy among the wives in those villages. First Wife was at the top, the woman most respected by the husband in a village. Her sons would become responsible for the village when the village head died. Being respected in the village depended somewhat on how many sons and daughters a wife bore to her husband.

A wife's relationship to her husband changed as her family grew. As a new bride she would be close to her husband. She would be responsible for his care and the maintenance of his house on a day-to-day basis. But after she had several children the village head would marry a new wife and the older wife would give more time to her children.

In this way the village was continually revitalized. The village head would now have a new wife to take primary responsibility for his care. He would continue to visit his older wives and they would continue to bear children. But they would also grow away from him as their families grew. In time, a woman's sons would be more responsible for her than her own husband was.

Mother was Sixth Wife in a village which grew to have about 15 wives. Mother's earlier children died, so her living sons were among the younger of Father's children. I was Second Son to her. With that position in a Luo family, my father normally would not have paid me much notice. I would have been close to Mother. But Father loved me and invited me into his house to milk his cows and to run errands, so my relationship to him was stronger than my relationship to Mother. Mine was a special situation made so because of Father's love for me. The focus of my childhood attention was on Father. I don't remember many specific things about Mother, just general memories.

Death was a common visitor in the 1920s and 30s. Ma-

laria and other childhood illnesses took many children. It
was not unusual for more than half of the children born to
die before the age of two. In Mother's house only four of her
10 or 12 children lived—all were boys. One of the remaining
four died of polio as a teenager, leaving only three. Because
there were no girls in our house, there was no one to help
Mother with the household duties. So Mother had to work
harder than most women.

A woman's life was hard, filled with work from dawn to
dusk. Twice a day, in early morning and late evening, Mother
set out for the lake, clay jar balanced on her head, to bring
water for her household. It was a mile and a half to the lake.
The water she brought was for cooking, and for washing
hands before meals and cleaning the cooking utensils. This
water was not for drinking, bathing, and laundry. Milk was
so abundant in our village that we didn't use water to drink.
We bathed and washed our few clothes at the lake. There
were designated places along the lakeshore—this place for
the cattle to come for water, that for women to bathe, over
there for the men.

Mother went far out into the lake where the water was
thigh-deep to fill her jar with clean water for domestic use.
That was the dangerous part of the lake because a crocodile
might be lurking in the scattered reeds that grew that
distance from shore. They would lie perfectly still in the
water—their long snouts looking exactly like pieces of drift-
wood. Today you seldom hear of crocodiles. They have all
been killed with guns. But 40 and 50 years ago there were
many of them, and women were often attacked when they
went into the lake for water.

We children looked to Mother for food. Let me tell you
about our food.

There are two parts to a meal, the *ugali* and the sauce.
In my boyhood the flour for making *ugali* was ground finger-
millet or sorghum. These are grains native to Africa.

Mother raised her own grain, as did the other women,
and stored it, unthreshed, in her granary. She would thresh
and winnow the grain as she needed it and grind it on her
large granite milling stone. Her grinding stone was
somewhat hollowed from many years of rubbing a smaller

hand-held stone on the larger one, slowly crushing red grain to powder.

Preparing the *ugali* required a hot flame under a clay pot half filled with water. When the water was boiling furiously, Mother scooped flour from her basket into the pot and stirred. Good *ugali* has no lumps of white flour in it, and it is so thick that it can be molded into a large lump. Skill and strength are required to knead the lump to the right consistency. The *ugali* must be kept so hot for the entire process that the cell structure in the flour is broken down—so that the grain is cooked. Raw *ugali* is troublesome in the stomach. The heavy wooden spoon would begin squeaking in Mother's calloused hands as the *ugali* thickened to ripeness.

Pure millet *ugali* (which I ate as a boy) is coarse and red. These days cassava has been introduced, and its flour is used by everyone to mix with the millet flour, making the *ugali* softer and somewhat pink in color. Today, millets have largely been replaced by maize, a grain Mother began to see only in her old age. Maize is safe in its husk from the quelea bird and doesn't need to be guarded when it is ripening in the field.

The second half of a meal was the sauce to season the *ugali*. In Father's village the sauce was prepared with milk or a milk product, yogurt or ghee. Mother cooked dried meat or lentils in this dairy base. The lake was close and it was easy to get fish, but Father saw fish as a poor person's sauce. Father didn't object to our eating fish, but he would have felt shame as a herdsman if any of his wives exchanged meat or ghee with the fishermen at the lake for fish. If Mother would have done this, Father could have beaten her or even dismissed her and sent her back to her father.

I loved to fish. For me it was a form of play. I often spent my free days fishing at the lake. I used a long tapering reed rod, my tiny hook baited with bits of earthworm, and I'd flick four-inch *furu* out of the shallows, taking them home to Mother. She prepared them for my supper, cooking them in milk sauce for my *ugali*.

Gathering firewood for cooking our meals was also Mother's responsibility. Every several days she would borrow a machete from one of her co-wives, take her leather cord and go into the savannah looking for dead wood. Sometimes she went in a group with women and daughters from other households in the village. This work was dangerous because it took Mother close to the thickets where there were snakes and leopards. When she had gathered several days' supply, Mother tied the wood into a bundle and, balancing it on her head, carried it home.

Mother was a good farmer. She was responsible to raise the millet which fed herself and her children. At the time of the year when the Pleiades appeared in the eastern sky, four months of drought would end. Rain would water the earth, turning its brick-hard soils soft. Then it was time to prepare the earth for planting.

Each of Father's wives had her own several acres on which she raised her millet. But they were not allowed to begin work on their own "farms" until after Father's personal field had been prepared for planting.

Everyone in the village worked together preparing Father's field. He set the day. The evening before, Mother prepared *ugali*, putting it in a small tightly woven, bowl-shaped grass basket. Early the next morning, at the first rooster crowing, she was up preparing the sauce. The whole village then set out for the place Father had chosen for his field that year. We used short-handled hoes, stooping to dig up the sod, turning it over. We knocked the clods about with the back of the hoe to smooth the field. Roots and weeds that didn't turn under would be pulled loose with the hoe and piled on a rock to die in the sun.

Father's task was to see that we were organized. He was responsible to see that everyone was working. He stood somewhat apart from the activity on a bit of higher ground or a rock. He stood there with his stick or sat back on his heels, watching us. We were afraid of him, and everyone worked steadily all morning.

At noon Father would call a halt to the work. Time for lunch. The youth ate together in one place. Their mothers took their food to them where they sat under a tree. Each mother then ate with her younger children. All the food had been prepared the night before. Sometimes smaller households would eat together, or if two wives were close friends they may have prepared their food together.

If Father wandered off during lunch break, very little work got done in the afternoon. But if he stayed nearby, he would soon call us back to work and we would work into the late afternoon. There were so many of us and we worked so well that one day's labor usually was enough to prepare a field large enough to satisfy Father.

After Father's field was prepared, then Mother prepared her own field. We boys helped her with the initial digging, but after that it was her task to plant and weed. At the harvest she stored the grain in her granary. We boys did take turns guarding the field from the quelea birds as the crop ripened for harvest, but the other tasks were hers to do.

As long as Father lived, he saw to it that cows were assigned to Mother's care even though she had no marriageable daughters. We had milk because of Father. We lived in the shadow of his wealth. When Father died, responsibility to feed us boys became solely Mother's burden.The rains didn't come properly in the late 20s and Mother got little from her field. It was then that she began to take trips into Kenya, to Kadem, going back to her brothers' villages. These people, my maternal uncles, would not turn her away in her need. She would be gone for several days, returning with smoke-cured fish, aid from her brothers to help us through those lean years while her sons were still young.

When I remember Mother, I feel a great reverence for her. If she were alive today, I would go to the lake and bring her a bucket of water. I remember her rising early and going to her field, coming home again in the 10th hour of the day with a load of wood on her head which she had gathered after weeding all day. Then she would be off with her jar to the lake for water. By dusk she was back preparing bread and sauce for our evening meal.

This was the division of labor in those days in Luo society. A mother's fulfillment was in providing for the needs of her sons. A daughter's fulfillment was in helping her mother. There were no daughters in our house, so all of the women's work had to be done by Mother alone. Mother performed her duty well in difficult circumstances, a quiet steady labor on her sons' behalf. In our Luo tradition she was accounted a righteous woman.

You cannot know if your mother loves you. Mother performed her duty as is proper for a mother serving the needs of her children, but how could I know if she had any special love for me her second son? One day something very special happened. Sometimes I go back in time, and in memory live again that day.

It is 1937. Mother is now old and is living as a grandmother in Otulo's village—Otulo of the fish trap, my older brother. I have become a Christian and I am married. I am studying at the Mennonite Bible School at Bukiroba some fifty miles away. I become very sick. I nearly die. Word of my illness reaches Mother. She thinks the messenger is using Luo courtesy, that he isn't telling her the truth. She thinks the messenger is afraid to say plainly, "Your son, Marwa, he has bidden farewell; the fever has taken him." Her ears hear the messenger say, "Marwa is sick; fever has gotten strongly a hold of him." She knows, "Marwa is dead." The messenger's half-truth speaking only of illness could not deceive her heart, "Marwa is gone."

Okech, my mother weeps. In her Luo way she grieves for her lost son. She has lived to see the survival of only two sons.

"Do not weep, Mother," Otulo commands. "Marwa is not dead. Quiet your silly old heart. See, he is coming. Tomorrow he will be here. He is recovered from his fever."

Mother sees me the next evening walking into Otulo's village. She sees me strong and well, walking with my wife, coming home from the school where I am studying. She sees me welcomed and taken into my brother's house, into Otulo's house.

I am sitting in a chair, weary, content. Mother comes through the door of Otulo's house. She's come from her house, her grandmother's house, her house there in Otulo's village. She has a calabash in her hand. Coming up to me she scoops a palm of watery herbal paste from her calabash, slapping my left forearm, right forearm, left thigh, right thigh—green-liquid-marked.

"Drink," she commands holding the calabash in both hands outstretched. I drink a swallow. She drinks.

"My son, Marwa, I wept for you. My heart deceived this old woman, telling me you had bid us farewell. I have anointed you to expunge that lie, to turn it away lest it become a prophecy."

My eyes are moist with joy. Mother loves me. Her years of labor in my youth were rooted not in duty but in love.

Death

Father died in 1924. I was only 12. It had never occurred to me that Father could die. He had been sick for about a week. It was a fever of some sort.

One day during his illness he called his older sons to his bedside. I was not present, but I learned later that he had called them so he could tell them of the places he had put his cattle. Cattle were his wealth and he didn't keep them all in our corral. Some of his cattle had also been lent to his brothers to help them with securing wives for their sons. Some of my half sisters had been married without Father's having received the full dowry. The balance was a debt to him. Father told his older sons about all of these arrangements concerning his wealth. None of this was written down. These records people kept in their memory.

The morning of the day Father died I was sent to Kamageta to call several of his daughters to come home. Kamageta was only some ten miles away to the east. When I got back from my errand at about midafternoon, I found the whole village in great consternation. Father's wives were all outside the village enclosure. They were walking about with their hands over their heads weeping loudly and hopelessly. Several of them had collapsed sobbing on the ground. Neighbors were already gathering and they were weeping too, especially the women. It struck me that I was hearing the heart cry of a country at the death of its king.

All the rest of the day, through the night, and the next day, people kept coming. The whole country up to five miles away gathered at our village. There were so many people that a child could easily become lost among them.

The Luo people bury the dead inside the village enclosure directly in front of the dead person's house, just a few feet in front of the door. If for some reason the dead person did not have a house, then a small house or hut is quickly built. The dead person is then buried in front of the newly built hut. The Luo believe there is life on the other side of death, but God has very little to do with that. It is the family which makes the final assessment of a life. The family gives a person his/her final identity. It is important that all the relatives, and neighbors too, go to the funeral. In this way the person's life, as lived on earth, is defined and valued and his/her life in the hereafter is assured.

As Father's body was lowered into the grave, the drums began their rolling dirge—rising and falling like the ceaseless rolling of waves onto the lakeshore, sighing and moaning, representative of the ceaseless circle of life, birth, bloom, infirmity, death, round and round, a dirge articulating the sorrow and despair deep in the souls of the scores of people cut adrift by Father's passing.

On the day of the funeral the family announces when *teng'o* will be. *Teng'o*, the traditional ceremony for cleansing the village, is still observed today. *Teng'o* is the time to do battle with that evil thing which caused the death. The village must be rid of this enemy.

Warriors come from miles around prepared for battle. Their faces and bodies are covered with war paint. Many wear the skins of fierce and brave animals to give them courage. Many wear ostrich plume headdresses. They come with their long-handled spears and war shields. They also come with their cattle.

The warriors try to frighten the cause of death out of the village. To do this there is much drumming. The warriors dash about shouting battle cries and pretending to be at war. They thrust their spears into the grass roofs of the houses. They pretend to stab at people too, but it is only a feint.

The warriors also try to entice the cause of death out of the village. This is done with the cattle. For the Luo people the greatest enemy has always been the cattle thief. So the warriors drive their herds of cattle over the grave of the dead person. Maybe the cause of death will see a beautiful cow or bull and will follow the animal out of the village. This was the original theory, but these days we think of it just as an honor to the dead that everyone's cattle are driven over the grave.

Father's *teng'o* was set for the day following his burial. All the warriors from miles around came to our village in full battle regalia complete with war shields, long spears and battle dress—ostrich plume headdress and war paint. Even the great Chief Amuko came carrying his big shield and long spear.

The warriors brought the cattle from their villages along with them to the battle. The cattle were driven into the village enclosure and run over Father's grave. All the while, battle drums were beating and warriors were dashing about, spear and shield at the ready, shouting and feinting, stabbing the air here and there, hoping to pierce the demon which had brought this great devastation into our village.

Following a burial all the people who came must be fed. Cattle are killed to provide food. Cattle for meat are taken from the corral of the village where the death occurred. Also on the day of *teng'o* many, many people need to be fed.

For some nights following the burial, it is important for all the close relatives to sleep in the village. If a woman died, the relatives stay at the village for four nights. If a man died, they stay five nights. This is to comfort the bereaved, to give them courage and strength in the face of the tragedy which has fallen upon them. These relatives must be fed.

Some relatives and close friends of the dead may live far away and cannot get to the village in time for the funeral. It is important that they too go to the village to express condolences as soon as they are able to arrange to do so. For weeks following the burial, relatives and friends will continue to arrive at the village. They will stay for several days and then return to their homes. These people too must be fed.

This is all part of how the Luo people give ultimate personhood and identity to their dead. It is the duty of the living to serve the dead in this way. It is an expensive duty and the herd of the dead person may be devastated, leaving little for the survivors to inherit.

In recent years, because of the coming of Christian ideas into our communities, you will see people coming to a funeral with an animal—goat, sheep or ox—as a gift to the bereaved family. Thus, in recent years, people share the burden of death. But when Father died, the burden of meat and flour was borne by the village herd and the village granaries.

In the years immediately following Father's death, his village slowly fell apart. New villages formed out of the old as my brothers' families grew and they set up their own villages.

Father's wives became grandmothers in their sons' growing villages.

Today the site of Father's village at Kirongwe is a millet field. A pile of stones still marks his grave. Knowing that he was buried in front of the door to his house makes it possible for me to accurately place where all of the nearly twenty houses in the village once stood. I can easily place the area of the cattle corral.

Mother was a widow for 14 years. She died in 1938 of pneumonia. In her illness she was cared for at Shirati by a missionary, Ruth Mosemann, in the missionaries' one-room hospital. They gave Mother a bed there. My wife and Otulo's wife took turns being with her around the clock. At that time, in 1938, there were no medicines on earth for pneumonia. In a few days God took her. Her life was summed up and her body was committed to the earth in the traditional Luo way.

Nyasaye Nyakalaga, God the Creator

I am five or six years old. It is early morning. I am sitting outside Mother's house on the logs supporting her granary. The morning is clear, cool; my black skin is soaking in the sun's early warmth.

I fall into a reverie. "Here I am sitting by Mother's granary," I muse. "How has this come about? How did I, Marwa, come to be a human being? How is it that I sit here feeling the warmth of the morning sun?"

The answer comes as an epiphany, "If God would not have been, then I, Marwa, would not have been. God is both the purpose (why) and manner (how) of my existence."

Not much was said about God in traditional Luo worship. For the most part faith and worship were related to the village. A village was peopled by a big family. In my case the village was my father, his wives, and their children. But a village also had members who were on the other side of the grave, the ancestors. We thought of the ancestors as the living dead. We even thought of the unborn as members of the village. It was important to bear children, thus releasing the unborn into the living part of the village family.

In the oral tradition of the Luo people, stories are told showing that in the beginning God often came to the village and concerned himself with the affairs of people. But for some reason God moved away and left people to fend for themselves. This is why faith and worship for the most part had to do with the relationship between the ancestors and the living members of a village. God wasn't such a great part of the village life because he was far away.

But the Luo name for God, *Nyasaye Nyakalaga,* is spoken often. *Nyasaye Nyakalaga* means God the Creator, the originator, the source.

If a woman was pregnant, people would say to her, "*Nyasaye osekonyi*—God has helped you." Or to someone who had escaped from a crocodile or snake, even to someone who was wealthy or had given birth, people would say, "*Nyasaye osekonyi*—God has helped you." That morning when I was sitting by my mother's granary the name of God and the sayings that used his name came together for me. It came to me that God is *my* reason for being, that beyond the village activity and relationships there is One in whom all things, all happenings, have their beginning and purpose— Nyasaye Nyakalaga.

Several years after my early morning "vision," Christian evangelists passed through our country. I was herding goats that day on the savannah some distance from our village. Several smaller boys were with me. There were two evangelists, both Luo men, walking along the footpath. They saw us and called us to come to the shade of a tree there by the path.

These were the first Christians I had ever seen. I didn't think of them as Christians. I thought of them as men of God. These two men sang the most beautiful song for us goatherds. The tune was strange and ethereal, a melody drawing us out of the dusty savannah, lifting us beyond the circle of knowledge and experience that was familiar to us. The words were in Luo, speaking of God; the music was like the wind whispering in the trees.

After singing, the evangelists preached to us. They read from a book which said that God loves people and that he sent his Son to the world so that any person could have eternal life. Any who welcomed God's Son into the circle of his life would have acceptance with God. They went on to read that all the people who make themselves enemies of God's Son will be destroyed in everlasting fire. This was a new kind of life and death they were talking about—a reality beyond the circle of the village and its concern with the ancestors.

The evangelists were on their way from the Seventh-Day Adventist church at Muhuru in Kenya, just to the north of our home. They were going to their church at Sidika, near Shirati, eight miles to the south. They went their way, and I with the other goatherds ran to round up our scattering goats.

The evangelists noted our interest in their message. In a few weeks they came again. This time they came to Father's village. They were welcomed into one of the youth houses at the entrance to the village. All the youth from our village gathered to listen to them.

That night the evangelists sang many of the songs having that sweet melody and told us more about God. The book from which they read was called *Muma Maler*—New Covenant. The Seventh-Day Adventist message that night was the same as their witness the day I first met them out on the savannah.

"God loves us and shows us his love by sending his Son to the world. God wants us to live in his ways. Those people who refuse to live in God's ways, obeying his commandments, will be utterly destroyed by fire. Those who follow God and are obedient to his laws will not die but will live forever."

They spent the night in Father's village sleeping in the youth house. The next morning they went their way.

Before World War I Seventh-Day Adventist missionaries from Germany evangelized along the eastern shores of Lake Victoria. They built a large mission station only a mile from where the Mennonite Mission was later built at Bukiroba. During the war the British army came into Tanganyika from Kenya, eventually occupying more than half the country. Of course the Adventist missionaries fled along with the other Germans who had been living in Tanganyika.

After the war the League of Nations made Tanganyika a trust territory under British administration. The German missionaries never came back and their mission stations fell down. But the congregations and some of the bush schools continued under African leadership directed by American Seventh-day missionaries from Kenya.

Two years after Father died, four of us from his village began to go regularly to Muhuru in Kenya on Saturdays to worship at the Seventh Day church there. Muhuru is not so far from Kirongwe, where we lived. We would go in the morning and return by evening. It was in 1926 that I first began to go to church. I was about 14 years old.

A present-day peasant village: The outer fence, interconnecting the houses, is missing but the inner corral remains. This is a small village having only five wives.

The Ligero Church Choir: The congregation's leaders, Emmanuel and Mrs. Oudu, are seated in the middle.

Youth

Journey Outward

*F*ather's death set me free. As long as he lived he was the focus of my life. I was content. But when he died, something failed; that happy life came to a dead end. I remember that he passed away the year my body was changing and I was becoming a youth. I was discovering that there was a world out there beyond the circle of Father's village and my boyhood pattern of activity. So, in any case, I was becoming aware of the outside world, but Father's death thrust me out into it.

At puberty, boys stop herding goats and begin to herd cattle. All the cattle of the village are herded together. The youth take turns following them about. During those long days on the savannah the older youth talk of girls and share with their younger pubescent brothers the mysteries of the ways of men with women.

A Luo youth is not ready to talk with the girls until his six lower teeth have been pried out. As I got older I began to hear comments about my still holding onto my boyhood. "Ha, Marwa is still a boy with all his little-boy teeth still shining in his mouth." Girls with whom I spoke were laughed at by their friends. "So you are still talking with children? I saw you today in conversation with that Marwa whose teeth are still all in his mouth." When I sat in the evening on the edge of the circle of youth, they would laugh, "You, Marwa, do not come too close for you are still a child." Thus pressure was built up to have my teeth out and become a certified youth.

All of us knew the village of the nearest tooth puller. One day I asked a friend to go with me to his house. When we got there he told me to take off my shirt. He sat me down on a reclining chair and told me to open my mouth. He then pried the prescribed six teeth out one by one. My friend was holding my shoulders and encouraging me to be brave and sit still. The tooth specialist had given me a length of stick to bite. It was placed crossways in my mouth behind the front teeth. The lower front teeth, those were the ones he pulled. He used a sharp pointed metal lever to pry them out, all six.

For several days Mother heated water and bathed my lower lip and jaw to cleanse the wound and reduce the swelling. For a week I didn't take my turn herding the cattle. And then I was a youth—no more snickers about Marwa clinging to his childish ways.

Luo girls also had their teeth pulled—the same as the boys. In some villages there was a ceremony connected with pulling the teeth. But in my case it was just something I had done one day.

After a boy's teeth were out, it became appropriate for him to talk with girls and to become familiar with them. This was the time that we young men got to know the girls. Small groups of us would make trips here and there to visit girls in other villages. It was during this time that the youth began to know the ways of adults. There was a fairly strict code of conduct regulating these relationships. For a bride to be found by her husband not to be a virgin was a shame and embarrassment, so brothers were particularly protective of their sisters. In many villages the girls slept in their grandmother's house.

For us Luos there is a very strict code of conduct as soon as there is talk of engagement. Discussion from then on is done through a third party. The engaged couple are not allowed to talk together. They are kept strictly apart until the wedding day.

But youth was more than just the time to get to know girls. It was also the time to explore the outside world. My closest friend during my youth was Zefania Migire. He was the son of my oldest living half brother, a grandson of First Wife. Zefania was a few years older than I, so, although in the family he was accounted my "son," in my early youthful exploits he was my leader.

We often talked about getting educated. We could see

that changes were coming to our country. It seemed clear that the time was coming when it would be very important to know how to read. We decided to check out the possibilities of getting educated.

Zefania and I hiked over into Kenya to the Catholic mission at Asumbi, where there was a school. We asked if they had a place where students from a distance could live while they were going to school. They didn't have any place to put us, so we went back home again.

Not long after my return from the trip to the Catholic Asumbi Mission, two men from the African Inland Mission came into our area. They were buying cattle for a new meat-packing company in Kenya. Because Father had died, Otulo, my older brother, was responsible for managing Mother's household. He had decided that one of us four brothers should go to school.

Otulo didn't think there was much use in getting me into school because I was already a youth. Otulo was sure that I was much more interested in girls than in books. He decided that our younger brother, Malaki, be educated.

Otulo talked with the cattle buyers and found that they came from the Ogada Mission, where there was an African Inland Mission primary school. Otulo persuaded the cattle buyers to take Malaki with them when they returned to Kenya so that he could go to school at Ogada Mission. Malaki was still young; he still had all his teeth, and was not interested in girls.

Mother didn't know of Otulo's plan to make a reader of Malaki. That evening Malaki did not come for supper. "Where is Malaki?" Mother asked. Soon she learned that he had gone to Kenya with the cattle buyers.

The next morning Mother was nowhere to be found. Otulo decided that she must have gone in the night to bring Malaki back home. He was alarmed, knowing that the Ogada Mission was beyond Kisumu, over 100 miles away. Mother had no idea where she was going. Even if she would have known where she was going, Mother would become lost in the vast stretches of open country between Kirongwe, our home, and Kisumu. Otulo sent me to find Mother and bring her back home.

Catching up with her was not difficult. I found her on
the bank of the Kuja River. "Mother, what are you doing here
so far from home?" I asked.

"Malaki has gone with strangers who came to our
country. I do not know where he is going. I must bring him
back. If I don't, I will never see him again."

"Mother, you must go back home. I will follow Malaki for
you. I will bring him home with me. See, I will do what you set
out to do."

My dear Mother—she was so worried about her sons.
But she listened to me and went back home.

I crossed the river and found Malaki. But by then I was
eager to taste the adventure on which my little brother had
set out. I wanted to go beyond the horizon. The promise of being literate beckoned irresistibly. So I kept my promise to
Mother and sent Malaki home. Then I took up his adventure,
now making it mine.

That night the cattle buyers and I came to Kadem, the
country of my maternal uncles, and I directed my companions to the village of one of my uncles. We entered and
spent the night. The next day we were in country I had never
seen before. We walked three more days, spending the nights
in villages along the way. Eventually we came to Ogada
Mission.

One of the cattle buyers invited me to stay at his house.
Soon I learned that it was the school holidays, and no
students were there. I became lonely in that strange place.
After a week I decided to go home. Very early the next morning, under cover of darkness, I slipped away, telling no one.

I was really only a boy, 13 or 14 years old. All day long I
walked alone along the roads and paths over which we had
so recently come. I was surprised toward evening to recognize the village where we had spent the night on our way to
Kisumu. Thus it was each night. I got food and a place to
sleep at each of the villages where we had stayed on the
journey out.

On the third day my way came off the footpaths onto a
road, straight and endlessly long. On the footpaths I had
walked long distances without tiring because always the end
of the path was just there not far ahead where it turned and I

couldn't see it anymore. Now the endless road, clearly visible, stretching over the hills far into the distance, unnerved me. I became filled with hunger. My legs were rubbery; my whole being cried out for food. I remembered that there was a market along that road.

My mind was filled with visions of milk and bananas and sweet potatoes, of millet gruel spiced with lemon, of bread and lentil sauce bathed in ghee. It was now the third day since leaving Ogada Mission. I had eaten only at night, walking 25 and more miles a day. I was empty-handed. The shirt I wore and my tattered shorts were my only possessions. I was forespent. I remember that day now as in a vision.

I begin to pray, "*Nyasaye Nyakalaga*, God the Creator, see me here, a boy on this endless road, a boy filled with hunger. A piece of money, *Nyasaye*, may my eyes see by the road a piece of money, a coin for food at the market."

I come in the early afternoon to the market. There is my relative! He is coming toward me; he is greeting me, amazed at seeing me so far from my home. My relative is a trader in the marketplace. He is taking me to the place in the market where the prepared foods are sold. A great mound of cooked sweet potatoes he buys for me. He moves on—a calabash of sweet millet gruel spiced with lemon he puts in my hand. I sit down at a small table, I eat, I drink. My eyes clear and my legs fill with strength.

That night I came again to my maternal uncle's village. The next evening I was home, back with Mother and my brothers.

I was becoming serious about wanting to learn to read. My second effort at getting into a school had almost worked out. In later years, as my efforts to get an education were repeatedly frustrated, I would remember how nearly I came to being a student at Ogada Mission. Had I begun to study there, I am sure I would have done well and I would have gone on to secondary school.

At that time there were two outstanding secondary schools in Kenya, the Alliance Secondary School at Kikuyu near Nairobi and the Maseno Secondary School, just north of Kisumu, not far from Ogada Mission. Almost all of Kenya's early leaders were graduates of one of these two schools. Of course, if I had found the school in session, I would most certainly have joined the African Inland Mission. I would have stayed in Kenya and married a Luo girl from there.

The Seventh-Day Adventists opened a bush school at Tobwe a few miles from Kirongwe. I enrolled. It was a day school. I walked back and forth morning and evening.

When Father died, Zefania's father, my half brother, the oldest living son of Father's First Wife, inherited the responsibility for Father's village. In 1929 he decided that he should move from where we were at Kirongwe to Shirati. This idea felt good to us of Kisare's village because Shirati was in the middle of Kiseru territory, the clan from which Father had come. The move south to Shirati wasn't very far, about eight miles along the lakeshore. We settled some two miles to the north of where Mennonite missionaries later built a mission station.

Not far from where we settled at Shirati, the Seventh-Day Adventists had another church and bush school where I continued schooling. There at Sidika near the Shirati pier, I finished third grade. That was as much education as the Adventists offered. Of course, by then I was nearly a grown man.

After finishing third grade, I decided to get baptized. I enrolled in the Seventh-Day catechism class. I soon found from my catechism lessons that to become a baptized Christian I needed to obey certain religious rules. Becoming a catechumen didn't change my life at all. It seemed that my teacher hadn't expected me to be changed. No confession of sin or evidence of a changed life was required of me. All I had to do was attend the classes.

In the catechism classes we were taught that the main thing to do is to worship God on Saturday. We were taught that this is God's will: that everyone worship on the seventh day. Those who worship on Sunday have on them the mark of the beast. Anyone who has been baptized as Seventh-Day Adventist and then stops worshiping on Saturday is piercing the eye of God. This was basically the requirement to be a member of that religion. If you wished to be a holy person, there were certain additional requirements about food, like not eating scaleless fish.

I wanted to be a "person of God," to know him, the Creator, and to walk in ways that would be pleasing to him. So I followed the teaching of the Seventh-Day people, even though I found it sterile, having no influence on my real life whatsoever.

Early in 1933 I was baptized. A missionary came from Kenya. He put up his tent under a tree near the church. It was easy for me to see that he was only performing a ritual. To him we catechumens were just a job to be done. He had no interest in me. I saw no reason to take an interest in him. This white man baptized me, with others, in the lake. We went one by one into the lake and knelt by the missionary who baptized us by dipping water with his hands from the lake and pouring it on our heads. This is how I became a member of the Seventh-Day Church.

I took a new name the day I was baptized. My new name was like a certificate for the white people and those who worked for them, a name they recognized, a name that could open doors for you. For my new name I chose Zedekia—Zedekia, son of Kisare—Zedekia Kisare. Many years later as I got more perspective on the meaning of names, I began to use Marwa again, the name Father gave me, in addition to my Christian name.

During the year I was a catechumen, my older brother, Otulo, became a businessman. Otulo's baptized name was Simeon. He and a friend pooled their money, went to Kenya and bought a machine for separating cream from raw milk. It was called a separator. They set up their business at Rwang'enyi some 12 miles south of our new village at Shirati. Simeon hired me to run his share of the business. Another young fellow was hired by Simeon's business partner. The two of us worked together.

The machine had a large metal bowl on top that we poured the milk into. One of us turned a crank that made discs whirr inside. Soon skim milk would begin to come out one spout while rich, yellow cream came out another spout. We gave the skim milk back to the villager who had brought it. We paid for the cream. Every morning a long line of villagers brought their milk to our little factory. They took the skim milk home. We stored the cream in a cool place.

Every several days we boiled the accumulated cream in a drum or large kettle. The slow boiling continued until the milk solids separated out of the fat. This rarefied butterfat or ghee keeps for a long time without spoiling. When ghee is used in cooking, it gives the food an exquisitely delicious aroma. We bottled it and sold it in the marketplace for a high price.

As soon as the Luo people see that someone has discovered a way to make money, they try to make money the same way. Soon other milk-separating stations were opened near us, and my partner and I didn't get enough cream to stay in business. Simeon sold his share in the machine and I moved back to Shirati.

This was my first experience in the business world. It lasted less than two years and in the end was a failure. This experience didn't give me much hope to become a businessman. But that year and a half marked a basic turn in my life.

For the first time I was on my own away from home. It was during that time that I was baptized and got my new name. There was a Seventh-Day Church there at Rwang'enyi, where I worshiped every Saturday, but I came back home to Shirati to be baptized. Among the youth who came from the Rwang'enyi church to witness my baptism was Nyaeri, a slim and beautiful young woman, whose father teased her about her interest in me.

Nyaeri, My Wife

When Nyaeri was a little girl, her father, Kimba, borrowed a great black bull from his neighbor. The bull was supposed to improve Kimba's herd, and this he did quite satisfactorily. Nyaeri and her sisters were afraid of the borrowed bull, for he was big and sometimes dangerous. But they also admired him and gave him a name, Odera Kadhore, which distinguished him from ordinary bulls.

Out on the savannah Nyaeri's big brothers would boast to other youth herding their father's cattle. They would boast of Odera's strength and temper. One of the sports on the savannah was to pit bull against bull in contests of strength and endurance. The youth would whistle mockingly at their bulls getting them worked up and angry. Old Odera Kadhore would paw the earth throwing up clouds of dust and bellowing menacingly. Head down he would lock horns with a bull from another herd. Pushing mightily he would throw his opponent off balance. Odera usually won in these contests.

One day when Nyaeri was seven or eight years old, word came to Kimba's village that Odera Kadhore's owner at Kirongwe had died. Kirongwe was twenty miles to the north. Nyaeri discovered that her neighbor wasn't Odera's owner. The neighbor was a relative of the dead man and that is how he happened to be in possession of the bull. Now that Odera's real owner had died, the bull needed to be taken to the *teng'o* ceremony.

Nyaeri was sure she would never see her favorite black bull again. If he went to the *teng'o,* surely he would be butchered to help feed all the guests. That evening Nyaeri and her sisters climbed up on the logs of their cattle corral to have a farewell look at old Odera Kadhore.

Nyaeri's older sister wanted to go too. She begged her big brother to take her along. She even promised to help carry his heavy battle shield. So the two of them went, leaving Kimba's village at the first rooster crowing, driving Odera Kadhore before them.

Late that night they returned, the black bull still in tow. On her sleeping mat Nyaeri eagerly listened to her big sister's account of the forty-mile round trip to the *teng'o* and back.

"There were so many cattle that many of them could not even get near the village," her sister told her. "It would be easy to lose a cow or bull in that swarm of animals. The man who died was Kisare, son of Mbayee," she continued. "He must have been an important old man to have attracted so many people and cattle to his *teng'o,*" she observed, as she fell into an exhausted sleep.

Nyaeri was 15 or 16 when my partner and I set up our milk separator near Kimba's village. I didn't know that there was anyone near Rwang'enyi, who was not from my relatives' village, who would remember Father's *teng'o* and recognize the name Kisare.

Kimba's herd was robust. He had many cattle. He had

more than enough milk for his household. He sent Nyaeri, his daughter, every morning with milk to the place where I was operating the separator. She greeted me shyly, with respect and humor.

Soon I began to look for her among those who came each morning. I could see her coming on the other side of the valley. She had only one dress, sleeveless with straps over the shoulders, white. From a distance I could spot her in that white, white dress, always clean, spotless, shining—Nyaeri with her milk jar on her head. When it came her turn to pour her milk into the separator, we would talk together. She was straightforward, a person of few words, honest and open. Her face was always cheerful. I began to imagine the joy of her living with me always.

Nyaeri means "an orderly person." [Years later in 1962 at Bukiroba she was affectionately given the nickname "The German," because she was strict and allowed no nonsense in her home.] Well-named, Nyaeri Akello was second youngest daughter of Kimba's First Wife. Kimba married only two wives; Musangya, his First Wife, had seven living children. The birth preceding Nyaeri was of twins who both died. This is why Nyaeri was given the second name, Akello—She Who Follows Twins. Among Musangya's children there were only two boys and five girls. Kimba's younger wife, Achola, bore only three children who lived, one boy and two girls.

Nyaeri's father was an alert man. His village lay by the path between the lake and the place where we were separating milk. Every day after work was over I would go to the lake to bathe and relax. Sometimes I would fish. Soon when Kimba would see me passing his village he would call out to his daughter, "Nyaeri, I see your friend. Don't you think you had better go to the lake to do the laundry?"

As we became close friends and began to think about marriage, it became improper for us to be seen together. We needed to communicate through our friends or relatives.

Kimba became aware that I was seriously interested in his daughter. His friends told him that I was a poor fellow. "He has no cattle," they said. "You will get nothing for Nyaeri if you allow this friendship to continue."

But Kimba was a wise and good man. He liked what he

saw in me. He told these people, "Even poor boys need to marry. Long ago I too was poor, and for Nyaeri's mother I could make a down payment of only one cow."

While Father Kisare lived he managed all the cattle transactions in his village. You could think of those big old villages as highly developed capitalist systems. The success of a village was partly good management and partly good luck. A man began his village by paying dowry for a wife. He gave cattle to his bride's father.

If cattle had been accepted by the wife's father, then the children she bore belonged to her husband's village. It was a form of prostitution for a woman to live with a man who hadn't given dowry to her father because her children wouldn't belong to the man she lived with. Any children she bore would belong to her father.

Bride wealth showed the husband's serious intent in taking this woman into his village; it insured that the families of both husband and wife wanted the marriage to be successful. Even today a man-woman relationship can not be stable without the exchange of dowry.

When a man married his first wife, the bride-wealth was usually arranged by his father. If there were a surplus of cattle in the village, paying dowry was not a problem. But the man's father remembered how he came to be in possession of those cattle. If he had the cattle because of the marriage of the bridegroom's full sister, then the dowry was quite straightforward. But if the young man had no full sister of marriageable age, then cattle needed to come from the marriage of a half sister. Oftentimes when cattle went out of one wife's household to help the son of a co-wife marry, that debt was called after a while. Some of these debts stood for a generation before they were called in. Sometimes dowry debts were never called in.

Occasionally when a man had no way at all to get cattle with which to marry, he would elope with his sweetheart. After a time he would return home. Usually the bride's father would then let the man keep his wife, but the bride-wealth remained a debt of the young man to his wife's father. If the man died before the bride-wealth had been paid, his widow and her children returned to her father's village. If bride-

wealth had been paid, the widow and her children went to
her husband's father's village or they went to the village of
one of her husband's brothers.

So, when a man married his first wife, he hoped for
sons to be born who could inherit his wealth when he died
and could pass on his name and his father's name. But he
also hoped for daughters because it was through daughters
that he could get cattle through bride-wealth when they were
married. These cattle he could use to repay the debt he had
in marrying, if indeed it was an arrangement where he had a
debt. Through this bride-wealth from his daughters, he
could also get wives for his sons. Of course, he also used the
cattle that were coming in to get a second and third wife, etc.,
for himself.

Once a man had four or five wives, and sons and
daughers who were nearing marriageable age, the village
economy came to a take-off point and grew rapidly. The head
of the village was then considered an elder and he was
treated with respect. His poorer relatives would come to him
to "borrow" cattle for marriage arrangements when they
didn't have enough cattle. In this way a wealthy village head
could help his poorer younger brothers or his poorer nep-
hews (only brothers' sons) get started with their village
systems.

That was how the economy of a village worked. I have
described it in some detail because with a few changes this is
how marriages still work today.

My father was very wealthy. He managed his village's resources well. He made it his business to see that his sons
married early. Father had set aside cattle before he died so
my older full brother, Simeon Otulo, could marry. In fact Simeon did not marry until after Father's death, but, because
of Father's foresight, he did not have a problem with the
dowry for his wife.

Father was not very old when he died, probably in his
seventies. He was still mentally alert at that time. When he
became ill and saw that the illness was unto death, he called
his sons and recited in their hearing all of his cattle debtors.
This is how we knew where we could go for help should we be
without cattle to get wives.

If my father had lived another ten years, I would have had no problem marrying. Actually, because he loved me so much and I was so close to him, he would have hurried to get two or three wives for me. By the time I would have been 22, I would have been well on the way to building my own village. I would never have gone to school or been baptized.

Well, as my situation actually turned out, Father had died and Mother didn't have any daughters so the only way for me to marry was to go to Father's debtors. With Simeon's help I got together 18 head of cattle to give as bride-wealth to Kimba, Nyaeri's father.

Kimba laughed at those who had tried to smear my name by saying that I was a poor fellow. He said, "See, Marwa has given me enough cattle. Let him marry my daughter Nyaeri."

(My younger brother Malaki got cattle with which to marry because a daughter of one of Father's other wives came to live with us in Mother's house. When she was married, we got cattle which were used for Malaki to marry. Thus, all three of us surviving brothers got wives.)

I married Nyaeri in 1933, several months after I was baptized. I had moved back to Shirati by then, the milk separating business having failed. Ours was a traditional Luo wedding. The cattle had been taken to Kimba's village and accepted. When all had been arranged, one of my half brothers, Nathaniel Gomba, went to Rwang'enyi with a goat as a special gift from me to Nyaeri's father. Nathaniel then came with Nyaeri, walking, the twelve miles to her new home at Shirati. A few people gathered to welcome her into our village and to wish her well.

Several days after Nyaeri came to Shirati, a group of girls from Rwang'enyi followed her to see how her new life was going. They found her cheerful and content in her new home. These girls stayed for two nights and I butchered a goat for them. Then they went home but one girl stayed for several nights longer, just to make sure that my wife was content. Then she too went home.

A few days later a messenger came from Kimba's village calling my mother, Okech, and my bride to go to Rwang'enyi for a great wedding feast. Usually the husband does not go with his bride to this farewell feast put on by her father. But Nyaeri's birth had been unusual in that she had followed twins who had died; so I was advised to accompany her as a special precaution that all would go well. Therefore Mother, with her friends, and Nyaeri and I went back to Rwang'enyi for the feast that sealed our marriage covenant forever.

Thus Nyaeri became my wife. My mother was so happy to have such a cheerful young woman in her home to help her with her domestic duties. Nyaeri's coming was like a rebirth for Mother.

I loved Nyaeri from the first day she greeted me when I was separating cream from milk. I have continued to love her; it is now fifty years. I know that she respected me and loved me too because her marriage to me was something she thought through carefully from the beginning.

She told me that she was attracted to me because she found me to be gentle and soft-spoken. She thought maybe at home I was loud and rude, shouting at people. So she asked friends to investigate for her what sort of reputation I had back at Shirati. She heard that everywhere I was the same as she observed me to be when I was working at the separator. She told me that she decided it would be good having me for her husband.

Nyaeri became pregnant and in the time of life she gave birth to a son, and I was filled with joy. I chose for him a Christian name, Joshua. He lived only a few days. He wouldn't nurse properly. Maybe he was born early.

From the time of Joshua's death, Nyaeri and I entered a period of great hardship. There simply were no resources anymore in our home, no cattle, no goats or sheep, nothing. Nyaeri's one dress had worn out. All she had was one piece of cloth with which she clothed herself. I had only my one pair of shorts and one shirt. It was a collarless shirt that had one button at the throat; I pulled it on over my head. At night we lay together on our narrow, slat bed using for our blanket the one piece of cloth which Nyaeri wore for a dress during the day.

What could I do? I was distressed and deeply embarrassed. Even today I am embarrassed to tell of this time of trouble. I had married a wife and now I could not care for her.

After marrying it is not good to go crying to your brothers for help in the day-to-day business of managing your village. I could not go to Otulo for help.

Young men from the Shirati area were going to Kenya to work for wages. There was a saying, "He's gone to Mombasa," meaning that the person had gone away to seek his fortune in a faraway place. It was easier for us Luo people to do this than for the Bantu people because in our traditional worship we were not so closely tied to the graves of our ancestors as were the Bantu. At that time Luo young men were beginning to find jobs in the towns all over East Africa.

Nyaeri and I talked about what to do. I had seen a great white ship on the lake, powered by engines in its belly. I was told the ship's home berth was in Kisumu, Kenya. We decided that Nyaeri had to return to her father's village. I would go to Kisumu and get work on the lake steamer. When I got my wages and would be able to provide for her, I would call her to come again and live with me.

I was so embarrassed that I would not go with her on her journey back to her father's home. She set out alone. Not far on her way she happened to meet Simeon on the path. He asked her where she was going. Simeon refused to let her go home dressed only in a cloth. He brought her back and ordered a new dress for her at the shop. It was a white dress. It cost one and one-half shillings, 37 American cents.

Simeon told me white people had settled on Katuru hill some two miles south of where we lived. He advised me not to go to Kisumu. "Try first to get work with these people. If that fails, then go to Kisumu." Nyaeri decided not to go home. She hoped that I wouldn't need to go to Kisumu.

The missionaries had announced that every month they would hire five people to work for them, five new people each month. I went on the day for hiring. The older man, Elam Stauffer, was sitting behind a table with his notebook open. He was writing the names of the new workers. A younger man, John Mosemann, stood in the background. I was very shy. I stood watching from under a little tree. Noisy men were crowded around the table. They were giving their names and credentials. Soon Stauffer had his five men for that month.

The next month I went again. I could not bring myself to go up to these white men, to talk to them, to beg them, "Please, work!" No, I could not do that. Again I stood silent under the little tree watching. Again Stauffer wrote the names of five men in his book.

At home Nyaeri gently laughed at me, "Others who were there for the first time today were given work. You have gone twice and still have not spoken to these people. You are truly a quiet person. You should have married Simeon's wife instead of me. She is so shy and never says a word. If she were your wife, you two could just go off and be quiet together."

The third month I went again. Again I stood silent under my little tree. It was impossible. I could never bring myself to ask these men for help. Then I saw Mosemann pointing at me, talking to Stauffer.

"He has been here before," Mosemann said. "Call him over."

The older man beckoned me to come near. "What is your name?" he asked.

I stood at attention, straight and tall, arms firmly down, thumbs pointing to the ground, "Zedekia Kisare," I said. My name was written in Stauffer's book, in a Mennonite book.

This was the beginning of a year of hard labor for me.

*Bishop Kisare, outside the Rwang'enyi Church, with the
piece of rail he hung for a bell in 1939.*

Labor

During those closing months of 1934 we built Elam Stauffer's house. It was built of poured concrete; all the outer and inner walls were of poured concrete from the foundations to the wall plate. It was a large house with three bedrooms, dining room, sitting room, office, pantry, bath, and hallway. Two screened porches ran the length of the house on the side toward the lake and on the side away from the lake. The house itself was a rectangle but with the porches it was square. It had a corrugated iron roof. Ceiling board separated the rooms from the roof.

All of the work to build the house was done by hand. We carried sand from the lake. That was two miles away. We carried the sand in a *karai*, a large metal basin, on our heads. Water was closer. We carried it from a pond about a mile away. We headed the water, in a *debe*, a square tin can holding five U.S. gallons. Kerosene and petrol were imported in these *debes*. When they were empty we used them for carrying water.

We crushed rock for the concrete under the big tree near where the church was built later. The concrete itself was mixed with shovels on the ground and carried by *karai* to the section of wall that was being poured.

Some of the material for building was not available locally. It would come to the wharf at Sidika by dhow, a small sailing ship. The wharf had been built by the Germans before the war. They had located an administrative post at Sidika. The wharf was about six miles from where we were building. The missionaries had transported their belongings by dhow when they first came to our country. Now the building material came the same way.

We carried the lumber and corrugated iron roofing sheets on our heads the six miles from the wharf up to the mission site. There was an old German who still lived at Sidika who owned a cart. The missionaries borrowed his cart to transport the extremely heavy cement which came in kegs.

Most of the work we did was piecework—Shs. /05 per *karai* of sand delivered (later raised to Shs. /10), Shs. /05 per *debe* of water, Shs. /50 per *karai* of crushed granite for concrete, and so on. Those of us not on piecework got Shs. 4/50 per month, which at that time in American money was $1.12.

The German who lived at Sidika near the wharf had advised the missionaries that wages in the Shirati area should be kept low. This advice fit the circumstances of the missionaries. For one thing the missionaries didn't have much money, and for another the money they did have wasn't theirs. It was the mission's money, and they were very, very careful how they spent it. Also, the missionaries were in a hurry to build and so they needed many laborers so the work would be completed quickly. By paying a small wage they were able to hire more people and the work moved ahead swiftly.

Many people worked. Even Nyaeri, my wife, joined the piecework laborers carrying timber from the wharf, sand from the lake, and water from the pond. We worked cheerfully with open hearts, not just for the money but because we all wanted to be a part of the new thing which was happening at Shirati in the heart of Kiseru country. From the day we began digging the foundations of Elam Stauffer's house on October 25, 1934, to the day they moved into it on January 9, 1935, was only 77 days.

Building that first house was so expensive that the missionaries decided not to build that way again. After that they built with sun-dried brick. Not until 1960 did they begin to build with cement again, and then it was cement block. Even today that first house is the only Mennonite house built of poured concrete.

During that first year of working for the missionaries, I

discovered that my wife, Nyaeri, had the gift of money management. From my wages I would give her money to buy tea, sugar, kerosene and other household necessities. She too was earning a bit of money from her piecework on the building projects. Quietly and without telling me she was saving *tongulos*. Back in colonial days the British brought coins from England that had holes in them. The copper 10-cent piece was big, about the size of an American half dollar. I guess the British made them with holes thinking we would string them together. I can imagine a British banker sitting behind his desk deciding on the proper shape of money for "natives." Make it large, make it heavy, put a hole in it for people having no pockets.

We nicknamed this large 10-cent piece *tongulo* for the sound it made when a merchant dropped one in his money box. One by one Nyaeri was saving them. One day she held out her two cupped hands and soberly handed me a pile of money. We bought a sheep with that money, the first animal in Zedekia's village!

From then on I gave her all the money I made. Whenever I went to the market to buy meat or vegetables, I would ask her for money and she would get what I needed from her secret hiding place.

Once in the 1950s she astonished me by giving me a Shs. 100/= note. That is an incredible amount of money. At that time Shs. 100/= was four months' wages! We used it to buy a kerosene pressure lantern. This astonished the missionaries. "Zed got a pressure lantern? How did he do that? Why, he can't afford the money for kerosene to run it!"

More recently, when our son Abner went overseas to school we had to pay for his air ticket out of our own resources. My wife brought to me Shs. 1,000/=, about a quarter of the money needed for the ticket!

Now in her old age my wife has stopped hiding money. She has begun to forget where she had hidden it. Once I found some money in a book where she had forgotten it. So she doesn't save money anymore. But every month I still give her the living allowance I get from the church. And even today when I go to market, she gives me the money from the place in our bedroom where she keeps it. God has given her this gift of making my allowance reach to the end of the month.

But I must get back to my story about the missionaries. We Luo people give nicknames to each other. A good nickname should have a core of truthful insight and an edge of humor. It tells you something about the person. Soon we gave names to the missionaries.

Stauffer we named *Obano* meaning The One Who Resists or The One Who Is Against It. This was because he resisted our ideas about what the mission should be doing. By naming him *Obano*, we were recognizing that as a leader Stauffer couldn't be pushed around, and it meant too that we thought he was too inflexible. The mission came with its goals and objectives quite clearly defined. Stauffer resisted anything that he thought would divert him from the purposes which brought him. We on the outside saw this as an unwillingness to listen, a deafness to our agenda. Our objective was to get on the inside of Stauffer's world and to discipline it into being a useful resource for us.

We nicknamed John Mosemann *Bwana Misawa*. He was a cheerful friendly person. He was always saying "Misawa" to everyone he met. *Misawa* means "hello" in our language. We have a lot of other greetings, too, such as *Oyaore*—The sun is rising; *Oimore*—The sun is setting; *Inindo Maber*—Have you slept? and so on and so forth. But Mosemann stuck to the simple *Misawa*—"Hi, there," always the same, whether in the morning or in the evening. Whether it was his first meeting with you that day or the third, his greeting was always consistently, "Misawa." So we named him *Bwana Misawa*—Mr. Hello.

Partly this was a compliment to Mosemann's friendly, open spirit, but it was also a joke about his inability to be more sophisticated in his greetings. Even today in the Shirati area small children shout cheerfully and repetitively to passing white people, *"Misawa, misawa, misawa,"* apparently taught by their mothers that white people have only a limited Luo vocabulary.

Before long the mission got a half-ton pickup truck. It soon became clear to us that the car was not for "native" transport. We nicknamed the car *Adongo Oher*. *Adongo* is simply a boy's name. *Oher* means "He who is loved," so the name meant "Adongo, he is loved so much no one may touch him." When people saw the missionaries going by in their car they would say, "There goes *Adongo Oher* carrying his guardians."

Stauffers soon moved to South Mara leaving the Mosemanns in charge at Shirati. The whole mission station was then nicknamed *Ka Bwana Misawa*—Mr. Hello's Place. This nickname for Shirati mission and hospital is still widely used. These days some people have dropped the *Misawa*, calling the Shirati station only *Ka Bwana*, which means The Boss's Place.

Both Stauffer and Mosemann liked me. Stauffer was studying Swahili, the trade language used throughout Tanganyika. Swahili uses a Bantu grammar. There is no similarity between Swahili and Luo. Luo is a Nilotic language. Mosemann was studying Luo.

I was already literate. I had finished three standards at the Seventh-Day bush schools. I knew both the Luo and the Swahili languages well. So the missionaries turned to me for help in language study and in translating when they preached. Because the Stauffers moved to South Mara, my relationship to Elam did not develop much until later. Those early years I worked closely with the Mosemanns.

John liked me because I was quiet and truthful. I stuck to my work even when no supervisor was around. In working for a white man everyone tries to get some extra advantage out of the relationship. One doesn't work only for the wages but also for the advantage of being close to money and power. We call this *kutegea*. It means to set a trap or snare so you can catch something for yourself. *Kutegea* is characterized by ingratiation and hypocrisy. It seemed to me that everyone was working to get on the inside track with these people. I stubbornly refused to play these games. I discovered that John and his wife, Ruth, liked it that way. With me there were no hidden agendas.

Both John and Ruth didn't like to see me working so hard as a laborer. I am stocky with wrestler's legs, but I'm not a very big person. I had never worked as a laborer before. They began to find other jobs for me to do. Once John had me

translate some Swahili books into Luo. Looking back, I am
sure that was just something he did to get me to use my
brain instead of my back. I never saw the book again.

The Mennonites held their first baptism service on
September 15, 1935, about a year after I began working for
them. The whole congregation walked the two miles to the
lake. Nyaeri, my wife, along with 14 others, was baptized. One
by one they went into the lake, knelt down, and were baptized
by Elam Stauffer.

I stood next to Elam, translating for him from Swahili
into Luo. While Nyaeri was on her knees, a poisonous water
snake swam past between her and me. We just froze, not
wanting to panic anyone. That day I was taken into fellowship, along with five others. In addition to the missionaries,
the Shirati Mennonite Church now had 21 members.

Nyaeri took Susana for her new Christian name,
Susana, wife of Zedekia, Susana Zedekia.

By the end of their first year at Shirati, the missionaries
were preaching on Sunday at a number of places in addition
to the main station. Those first 21 members represented
several worship places, places where small congregations
were already gathering regularly. After the baptism, elections
were held to choose representatives or elders for the Shirati
District Church Council. I was a member of that first church
council.

Soon John Mosemann told us in the church council
that more Mennonite missionaries had come. Among them
were teachers, John and Catherine Leatherman. A second
mission station was opened south of the Mara River at
Bukiroba, near the town of Musoma. Farther south along the
lake among the Jita people congregations that had belonged
to the African Inland Mission were transferred to the Mennonites, and a second church council was formed in Jita
country.

In just a few months John Leatherman was pushing to
open a Bible school. The church council at Shirati agreed
that the new school should be opened at Bukiroba, a central
place midway between the growing congregations around
Shirati and those among the Jita people. Six of us were accepted to take the three-year course at this new school.

There were no students in that first class from South Mara. All six of us were from Shirati: Zefania Migire, Yakobo Agwanda, Samuel Ngoga, Daniel Opanga, Zedekia Kisare, and Thadayo Makori. (Thadayo later dropped out because of his brother's death. He had to go home to manage his brother's village.) School opened on October 14, 1936.

We had to walk to Bukiroba. By that time there were two half-ton pickup trucks on the mission, *Adongo Oher* at Shirati and another one at Bukiroba. But the cars were not for us. So we walked, Susana and I.

Earlier that year God had blessed us with a second child, a daughter. We named her Margaret. Now we carried Margaret with us in her little crib. I carried our bundle of possessions on my head; Susana carried Margaret's crib on her head with Margaret inside. Fortunately for Margaret, her mother never stumbled.

When Margaret would get fussy we would stop and Susana would nurse her. Sometimes I would carry Margaret and Susana would carry our possessions, taking turn about. I went ahead, Susana following, bundles on our heads, two people on the footpath walking to school.

The first day we followed footpaths still in use today little changed from 50 years ago. Passing through Omoche and Kirogo, crossing the Mori and Nyaburongo rivers, we would come by evening to the main road at Buturi. Susana's older sister and her husband lived at Buturi. We would spend the night with them.

Following the footpaths, Buturi is 21 miles from Shirati. It is much farther following the main road because it goes far inland in order to cross the Mori River in the hills where the river's course is narrow and a bridge had been built. The footpath crossed the river near its mouth close to the Mori Bay. Here the river is contained in the dry season within a deep crack, some 50 feet wide, snaking through a vast plain of black clay.

In October the river was low and we crossed on a wooden footbridge supported by tree trunks dug into the riverbed at a time the water was exceptionally low. During the rains we could cross at that place on a raft pulled by ropes held by people on either side. When there was a lot of rain, the whole plain would flood, and we had to go downstream and cross the Mori Bay in a canoe.

On the second day of our journey we awoke very early, at the first cock crowing, in order to cover the eleven miles from Buturi to Kinesi in time to catch the 9:30 a.m. ferry that crossed Mara Bay to Musoma. This second day we walked along the main road. The ferry, which had an engine, took us across six miles of water to the big town on the other side.

We then had another six miles to walk to get to Bukiroba, where the school was being opened. That was a long, tough, two-day 38-mile hike. The going would get particularly difficult as the day wore on and the morning coolness gave way to mid-afternoon's airless, baking heat.

During the shorter school vacations, I would walk home alone, leaving Susana at Bukiroba with Margaret. The trip was just too hard for her. But on our longer vacations we would travel that way together.

In our second year at Bukiroba she was pregnant again. That time we came home by dhow. This third child, a boy, Clement, was born at Shirati. He died shortly after birth.

At Bukiroba our life of hardship started all over again. There were few buildings built by that time, so three of us students with our wives were housed in the car garage. This building had two rooms separated by a wall without a door. The smaller room was a tool shed. We didn't have access to that.

The larger room was just big enough for the station pickup to nicely fit inside with room on one side for stacked lumber. The side opposite the lumber had large windows. This longer of the two rooms was open up to the roof. The smaller room on the end of the building had a sturdy plank ceiling. By climbing up a ladder fastened to the dividing wall, we could get up on the ceiling that covered the smaller room. There under the roof two couples made their bedrooms, one to the right and one to the left under the eaves.

Because Susana and I had Margaret with us, we were given the room where the Ford was parked. The only place there big enough to spread our reed mat was in the bed of the pickup. So the pickup bed became our new bedroom at Bukiroba.

The three women cooked in a little hut outside the garage. We went to the lake, half a mile away, to launder our clothes and bathe. We carried water by *debe* from the lake for our domestic use.

At school each of us students earned Shs. 5/= ($1.25) per month. This we used to buy food and any other thing we needed. Since we were out of our home environment, getting food became more difficult and expensive than it had been at Shirati. I often went hunting with my knobkerries for rabbit, quail, and guinea fowl. Fish were often available at the lake where we bought them from fishermen. I remember one day when we had no meat for sauce I got a quail with my throwing stick, one little *aluru*, which four of us couples used together that night as sauce for our bread.

We had classes in the morning and we worked in the afternoon to earn our monthly Shs. 5/=. Much of the work was piecework. A particularly difficult job was carrying water from the lake for the missionaries' rainwater tanks and for building work. We had to do this only during the dry season when there was no rain collected off the corrugated-iron roofs of the missionaries' houses.

When the assignment was to carry water, the set piece of work was 12 *debes* carried one at a time from the lake, a one-mile round trip. In order to get this done in an afternoon we ran down to the lake and walked back up heading the full *debe*. The set piece of work for cutting grass was one acre. My head often ached. I became very weary of this endless work.

Sleeping in the bed of the missionaries' car also had its problems. Sometimes our teacher would take the pickup in the late afternoon, forgetting to remove our bedding. Usually such trips were to Mugango, the third Mennonite mission station 25 miles away toward Jita land. Elam Stauffer lived on the Mugango station and our teacher would go to consult with him. The car would come back late at night. We had to sit up waiting for its return. When the missionaries went hunting and got back after dark, we had to wash out the truck bed and dry it with grass as best we could before making up our bed for the night.

On February 16, 1937, during the second term of my

first year at Bukiroba, Catherine Leatherman gave birth to a daughter, Lois. Two years earlier Elizabeth Stauffer bore a daughter who did not live. So this daughter of Leathermans was the first white child born in the mission. The missionaries felt it was important for the news to reach their fellow missionaries at Shirati. I was sent on the four-day trip by foot to Shirati and back to take the news of this event.

Looking back on these experiences, I do not blame the missionaries for these hardships we endured. We were all so eager for an education that we willingly put up with great difficulty. John Leatherman, in particular, within the colonial boundaries which defined our relationships, was a fair man. He was also a passionate man. This was how God created him, full of adrenaline.

We quickly nicknamed him *Oleche*—He Whose Veins Throb. He was of German background. John had no favorites among us, and he never did anything for spite or looked down on us for being poor. Leatherman had the gift of discernment; he would judge an issue rightly without favoritism.

Before long, Leatherman became aware of my teaching gift, and whenever possible he would use me as a teacher; in this way he reduced my time in hard labor. We came to honor and respect each other. He was always especially courteous to Susana. Maybe that was because we slept in the bed of his little truck during that first year before the students' houses were built. Sometimes he would send her greens for her cooking pot.

All five of us students had hoped that our education at the Bible school would count toward additional secular education. But the missionaries wouldn't budge on this point. They had no interest in giving us an education beyond the ability to read, write, and do simple sums. Preaching the gospel was the mission's objective, period. During the three years we studied at Bukiroba, Catherine regularly taught us special courses to bring us up to the education level of Standard 4. This was judged to be all the secular education needed by a preacher of the gospel.

The core courses at Bukiroba were the standard Bible school curriculum—Old Testament, New Testament, Church

History, Doctrine, Church, and Leadership. I found Catherine Leatherman's Old Testament courses particularly interesting, for I found so many parallels between our Luo society at Kiseru and those ancient people of God.

During the last of our three years at Bukiroba, Susana gave birth to our second daughter, Miriam.

Near the end of my studies I went one day to the missionaries' workshop and asked for a three-foot length of heavy locomotive rail. It weighed about 40 pounds. I asked the missionary to drill a hole in the one end so I could put a stout piece of wire in to hang up the metal.

"What is this for, Zed?" he asked.

"For a bell to summon students and worshipers."

The pleased missionary put it in the pickup and transported it for me to Shirati.

A month after I returned to Shirati, at the close of my studies, the Shirati Church Council assigned me to open a bush school at Rwang'enyi, Susana's home. We moved with my "bell," that heavy chunk of rail, so different from the machine for separating cream from milk that had taken me there seven years earlier.

In 1983 the rail is still in regular use, somewhat flattened at one end from countless bangings. It is hanging there in a tree outside the Rwang'enyi Mennonite Church.

The Shirati church: This church was built by John Mosemann. In 1940 it had a grass roof.

Blood

*I*n those early years of my association with missionaries I was a fool; probably I am still a fool. We saw the missionaries as being very powerful because they had education, money, and equipment. They not only had these things; they knew how to get them.

We wanted these things too. In order to get on the inside of the missionaries' system many of us tried to act in ways that would please them, do things their way, agree quickly with how they saw things. This way we hoped that they would come to like us and that it would bring us closer to the secret of the power they had.

People who "played the game" often found the missionaries generous in helping them with life's day-to-day problems. The missionaries would give responsibility in the work of evangelism and teaching to the people they liked and trusted. People obtained employment, too, from the missionaries, such as work in the hospital. They opened doors for you if you made yourself pleasant to them. I say that I was a fool because I refused to play these games with the missionaries.

Those of us who were working with the missionaries at Shirati in the early 1940s came from five villages or extended families. Each of these five families was big, like my father's family. You might almost consider each of these families as a clan. Of my father's many sons, six were working in one way or another with the missionaries at Shirati.

The first person to be hired by the mission to work in the dispensary that was opened in 1934 was Nathaniel

Gomba. He was one of my father's sons, my half brother. We sons of Kisare looked out for each other. As I said, there were five villages or families represented on the Shirati station in those early years. These five sets of relatives struggled against each other to be in top favor with the missionaries.

In our Luo society the purpose of man is to build up his father's village or family. Within a family we recognize each other, *tunatambuliana*. It is my duty, and joy, to build up my brother because this builds up our father's village. To recognize someone is to see him as a person, to care about and help him, to hurt when he hurts and to be happy when he is happy. We recognize only a person from our own clan or village.

Girls are married from their father's village into another village. A wife's duty is to bear children to build up her husband's village. A woman does not build up her father's village but her husband's village. This is one of the reasons why a man gives bride-wealth to his father-in-law.

Our traditional worship was concerned with building up the village. It was important that village ancestors, two and three generations back, were pleased with our lives. From time to time we made sacrifices at our ancestors' graves so they would know that we were respectful of them and that our lives were being lived in such a way that their village was being strengthened.

Sometimes in our society there would be a hero who would be recognized or respected outside his father's village. An example is the wrestling, *mwereka*, hero. From time to time youth from various villages would get together to wrestle. If one of the wrestlers couldn't be beaten, then he was a hero and he would be recognized by all the villages.

A modern example of this is the soccer hero. My son Abner went to America and he came to be recognized by many people because of his soccer ability. Such a hero we call "iron"—*chuma*. Our people take great joy and pride in someone who has exceptional strength or skill. Such a person is encouraged and helped by everyone, even by people who are not his relatives. Because of his outstanding gift, he is recognized across the country in many villages.

But normally, in our society, we helped only our relatives, people from our father's village. So in those early days at the mission there was a lot of competition between families to get on the inside with the missionaries. It was a normal thing for people to spread gossip and bend the truth when talking to the missionaries about workers and church members who weren't from their village. The missionaries were hearing a lot of things, but I don't think the missionaries really knew what was going on.

Our definition of gossip, *masengenyo*, is talking about another person in such a way that he gets a bad reputation. If you know something true about a person, you can talk about it in two ways. The first way is to tell it in such a way that the person you are talking to will be sympathetic to the person you are talking about. The second way is when you want the person to whom you are talking to be suspicious of and to despise the person you are talking about. This second way of talking about another person is what we call *masengenyo*.

In the traditional village, *masengenyo* was not allowed. It was wrong to gossip to someone outside the village about a member of your village. But it was all right to gossip about someone from another village. It was important to build up the reputations of your brothers and fathers, or the reputation of a hero. But there was no reason in our Luo society to build up the reputation of anyone who did not belong to your father's village.

The missionaries were no different from us. Their Shirati compound was a village of white people. These days people are careful how they talk about outsiders who don't belong to their group, *wamestaarabika*. We are courteous in how we talk about others. We have studied psychology. But back then people from the West had a colonial mentality. Back then the colonialists would not accept us unless we became Western in our way of life. The only way for an African to become respectable in the eyes of a white person was to dress and act and live like a white person. This is what I mean by the colonial mentality. The missionaries had this mentality too. They thought of us as "native"—*wenyeji*.

The principal way in which the missionaries kept us out of their white village was by refusing to help us to get

educated. They considered three or four standards of education all that was necessary for a "native" to be a good church
worker. They taught us the Bible and church history and
theology many times over, but they saw no need for giving us
more than just a taste of geography, commerce, science,
mathematics, administration.

Their standard answer to our pleas for education was
that they had come to preach the gospel. They said that if
they gave of their time to educate us, then they wouldn't be
preaching the gospel because there wasn't enough time to
preach and educate. If they were not preaching the gospel,
then they had no business being in Africa. Therefore, giving
us an education, they told us, would be against the plan of
their mission and they would have to go back to America.

We pleaded for them to teach us English if they were
unable to give us a general education. But they refused, saying that we had no need for English. "You cannot preach the
gospel to natives in English," was their conclusion to the
matter.

Even today it would be easy for me to be bitter about
this. We couldn't get inside their village. The colonial standards they set for us couldn't be met if we couldn't get more
than four standards of general education and if we didn't
know English.

In those early years the missionaries held a conference
every year. At their conference they elected mission officers
and set mission policy for the next year. Especially important
conferences were held when leaders came to visit from their
church in America.

In those early years of the mission, no African was
allowed to attend these conferences or to see the reports. Of
course, all the meetings were in English, the inside language
of their village. It is true that the missionaries had organized
church councils on each mission station to decide on the
issues of each of the church districts. By 1942 there were five
of these church districts, one for each of the five mission stations. Africans were elected to these church councils, but the
mission set overall policy and those doors were closed to us.

It was not possible to work together this way. I believe
this is why John Mosemann quit after only one term of ser-

vice, although he told us it was for health reasons. He went back to America in 1939. He did not have this colonial spirit which tried to keep us in our place. John from the beginning was a man of God. He could not accept the spirit with which many of the other missionaries approached Africans.

During my three years at the Bukiroba Bible School, I read my Bible through many times. Slowly I began to see that in Christ my wife Susana and I were equal before God. During the first years of our marriage I insisted on having the last word in our home. We fought, Susana and I. I struggled to make her an obedient wife. Then I saw from my study of the New Testament that a husband and wife are to work together. All our quarreling ceased.

I began to go to the lake to bring Susana water. In my father's village no man carried anything on his head. Heading was for women. A man carried things on his shoulder not his head. But you cannot carry a *debe* of water on your shoulder.

When we were carrying water from the lake at Bukiroba to fill the missionaries' rainwater tanks, we carried the *debe* on our heads. That was all right because it was Western work we were doing for a white man. But putting the *debe* on my head and carrying water from the lake for my wife to use in my home, this simply was not done by Luo men.

People laughed at me when they saw me carrying water for Susana. They said that I was ruining my wife. "She will become uppity," they warned. "She will become like a white woman telling you what to do."

But I continued to relate to my wife in this new way that I had seen in the New Testament. How I related to my wife was the practical outcome of my realizing that in Jesus Christ we are of equal value before God. In this way Christianity was making a difference in my life. It was several more years before my faith began to make a differnce in how I related to the missionaries and to Africans who weren't from my father's village.

I was happy to have been assigned by the Shirati Church Council to open a bush school at Rwang'enyi. This was an out-of-the-way place, far from any road, ten miles from the struggle on the main station that was going on between the various ethnic groups there. If you measure things the way the world measures them, you would say that I was a fool. I had no stomach for these things, and still don't. How could I become a leader without jumping into the struggle to be first? But I prefer to live on the edge of things where it is quiet. I think I got this characteristic from my father.

I was a fool for a second reason. I was not afraid of the missionaries. I saw that they did not accept us Africans as equals, so I despised them. You could say that I hated them. I knew that I was intelligent. I knew that I understood the basic issues. I was proud to be a man of Kiseru, a son of Kisare. I didn't try to hide my pride.

It is a strange thing with me. On one hand I am a timid person. Where people are struggling to be important, I prefer to keep at a distance. Yet, when I see injustice, something inside forces me to speak out.

Once in a church council meeting one of the missionaries was especially impatient with us. "Can't you see, you stupid fools?" he demanded.

I stood up at once and read Matthew 5:22: "Anyone who says, 'You fool!' will be in danger of the fire of hell."

The missionary bit his lip and lowered his head. "I am sorry," he said. "Please forgive me. I should not have spoken that way."

"I forgive you," I answered.

This is how it was in the church council where I was an elected member. I became known as the one who would tell the missionaries what he thought. The African members were happy to have me do this. What needed saying got said, and they hadn't hurt their reputations with the missionaries.

After a meeting where I had spoken out, they would give me encouragement, "Well said, Marwa! You say it like it is." In this way, because of my boldness in speaking out, I was not well liked by the missionaries and I missed out in a number of ways.

By 1942, eight years after the missionaries had come, things were not going well at all in the church. That year I was moved back to Shirati from Rweng'enyi. The man who had been teaching the bush school at Shirati, Zefania

Migire, went to Bukiroba to take his last year of Bible school because he had not finished with the first class of graduates. I was transferred to Shirati to take his place during the year he was away at school.

Elam Stauffer, our bishop, was an alert leader. He knew that things were not going well in the church. He knew that as a missionary he was far away from us. His leadership was broken. He knew we were gossiping about each other, that we were full of hypocrisy, that there was sin among us, that there was no love in the church. He couldn't help the situation. We couldn't help him.

Stauffer heard that God had brought blessing in Mwanza to the African Inland Church, so he went to Mwanza. He went to Emil Sywulka, the A.I.C. missionary who had come with Elam and John Mosemann on their first trip into Mara Region back in 1934. Sywulka had helped the Mennonites to find the place to put their first mission station. Sywulka was a great man of God. The people in the Mwanza area had given him the name "Praying Shoes" because the toes of his shoes turned up from the many hours he spent on his knees in prayer.

Something happened to our bishop in Mwanza. He saw himself. God's light from heaven shone on him and he saw his Swiss-German self-righteousness. He saw that the way to freedom is to repent of his self-righteousness. He saw that the blood of Jesus from that sacrifice on the cross can set people free, bringing them into a new relationship with God and with each other. Our bishop, Elam Stauffer, came back to us at Shirati changed. He was a free man. He saw us differently from the way he had seen us before.

In the church council we decided to have a spiritual life conference that year for the whole Shirati district. The members from all the small bush congregations would come to the Shirati station for two days of meetings. We would have the conference on Saturday and Sunday, August 8 and 9.

In May we began to have early morning prayer meetings in the Shirati church. This was an important preparation for the conference. Every morning we got up at the first streaks of dawn and went to the church to pray. After the sun was up, we disbanded again and went about our normal daily duties. This we did for three months, every day.

The conference was just us, the members of the Shirati district. No outside resource people were there to preach. We began with prayer and then for two days Stauffer, and others, preached.

The preaching was in Swahili and translated into Luo. I did a lot of the translating for that conference. We preached with heavy hearts, knowing that God was not pleased with our situation at Shirati. We realized that we had nothing to be joyful about.

On the morning of the last day of the conference we knew that this day God would visit us. In the morning we again had preaching. After lunch we gathered in the church for the last session of the conference. We had no preaching. Stauffer spoke a few words. His heart was heavy, yet we could see that he had great inner peace. He asked us to pray.

We began to pray, one at a time. As we were praying this way, there came a moment of silence. No one told us to be silent. It was simply that we had nothing further to say. It was a heavy silence, the silence before a storm.

Then a great cry burst from every heart. In a moment the whole church was filled with weeping. It was as when you strike a match to petrol; suddenly with a great whoosh the whole congregation was struck down! It was like the explosion when the sizzling fuse ignites dynamite, whoom! It was like the cry at the death of a king, everyone in a moment weeping out of the empty lostness of his soul, "Woe, woe is me! for I am undone."

The weeping continued for an hour without letup. Bishop Stauffer was wise to allow the weeping to go on. At last he said to us, "Speak now. Why have you been weeping? Tell the congregation."

Up to that time we had never admitted our sin to each other. Each covered his sin, keeping it to himself, pretending to others that he had no sin. But that day we spoke each one of our sin. Each person confessed what it was that was keeping him or her from being in a good relationship with other people.

As we confessed, our self-righteousness melted before one another. Freely we confessed to one another, asking forgiveness; freely we gave forgiveness to each other. We experienced no shame to do so because we felt Jesus' great love for us. The blood of his sacrifice on the cross took away the sin and jealousy and pride and self-righteousness that had made us enemies of each other, that had kept us from working together.

Our time of confessing to one another, of receiving forgiveness, of being set free, continued until dark. Lanterns were brought. No one thought of food. Finally at 9:00 p.m. there was silence again, the silence of peace. We prayed and then went to our places for the night.

The next day all those people who had come from so many different places around Shirati went home. Everywhere we went we began to straighten up our lives. In the traditional faith of the Luo people, the shaman used to come to straighten up the village, to put everything into a right relationship. This is what was happening; only it was Jesus who was putting everything into a right relationship.

We on the Shirati station set about straightening up our lives both among ourselves, African and African, and between ourselves and the missionaries. It was a time of great joy and freedom. Bishop Stauffer and I came to love each other. We respected each other, and each gave to the other the honor and place which was his due.

What was happening at Shirati was not strange to anyone who understood the traditional Luo faith. In our village life we support each other; we look out for each other; we work to build up the strength of the village. If a village member sins, we still support him.

But it is possible for someone to commit so great a sin that covenant is broken between him and his father's village. Suppose a young man kills his brother, someone from his own village. Suppose a young man sleeps with one of his father's wives. Suppose a man sleeps with his own mother. These are terrible things. It is no longer possible for this man to live in his father's village. He is thrown out, *odhi bue.* Usually when someone is caught in such a sin he will run away himself. His sin chases him away. This man has no people; he has no village; he is outside of the village covenant, lost.

When someone is thrown out of his father's village, he can not return. He may stay out for 40 to 50 years. But the time will come when he will become old and he will not want to die outside without a family. So he will send word to his father's village asking to be accepted again by them.

No matter how good a man he may have been or how much the people of the village may have admired him, it is never possible for him to return unless a sacrifice is made which is powerful enough to undo the evil thing which he did. We know in our society that only the blood of a sheep killed in ritual sacrifice has the power to break the curse which that man brought upon himself when he sinned against his father and his village.

The date is set for the return of the sinner. A low opening is made for him in the village wall, at the far end, opposite the village entrance. Before the lost son may enter the village, a sheep is killed. The sheep's blood, along with juices from the small intestine, and certain herbs are mixed together. The lost person then confesses fully the evil thing which he did against his father and the village.

After he has confessed, he is symbolically cleansed. This is done by sprinkling him with the prepared liquid. He drinks some of it. He then stoops down in humility and enters the village through the low entrance that was made for him. After he is on the inside of the village enclosure, more cleansing ceremonies are performed. Then he is taken to a small hut, prepared for the occasion where he eats with members of his father's village.

The only way to restore a broken covenant is (1) confession of the sin which caused the covenant to be broken and (2) the sacrifice of a sheep whose blood removes the curse that stood between the sinner and his father's village.

We believe that sin, that which brings a curse on a person breaking covenant between him and his village, can be knocked off only with blood after confession. We say in Luo, *"Ja chien idolo giremo*—Satan is neutralized only with blood."

To sin is like a person taking hold of a live electric wire. His arm is in spasm and he cannot let go of the wire which is killing him. Anyone who catches hold of him to help him will also be gripped by the current and made helpless. Only by taking a piece of wood can the live wire be knocked from the man's grasp. This is the work of blood in our society; blood alone can knock off the evil which is grasped by a person or village.

That August evening in 1942 the Holy Spirit gave us the insight that both the missionaries and the Africans were all lost from that one true village, the new village of God our Father. It was sin which kept us concerned only with our own earthly families, our ethnic villages. The Holy Spirit showed us that Jesus' sacrifice made it possible for all of us to be brothers and sisters in the same village.

At first I could not accept that God wanted me to become the brother of the missionary, that God wanted me to account the missionary to be of the same village with me. How could I accept that, when I felt the missionary's own ethnic pride so keenly?

The Holy Spirit also showed me that I must honor and respect as my brothers the Luo people on the Shirati station who were not from my father Kisare's village. How could I accept to do this when I knew all about the gossiping and hypocrisy which stood between us as we struggled for place with the missionaries?

But that evening we all saw Jesus. By that I mean that we saw the crucified Lamb of God whose blood removes the walls that separate people from each other and from God their Father. A great light from heaven shone on us and each saw his own sin and each saw the new village of God. We all saw this revelation together, so it was easy to confess to one another and to forgive one another.

We now saw each other in a different way. Earlier such things as theft, adultery, lying, malicious gossip, and jealousies were not so bad if they were directed against people of another village. But if we were all members of the same new village, then we needed to hold the character of each other person as sacred. We needed to ask forgiveness and make things right even with those of a different ethnic background.

People who have not met Jesus don't understand this.

They don't realize that without Jesus' sacrifice the church would not be possible.

It was only because of Jesus' blood that Elam Stauffer and I were able to recognize each other. Without that sacrifice he was nothing to me. If he was just an ethnic Mennonite holding to the ways of his Mennonite ancestors, holding to his Swiss-German heritage, then he was no different from what I was when I held to the ways of Kisare's village. My ethnic heritage was as rich and meaningful as his.

An ethnic heritage may be a blessing to us. But there is no salvation there, no new village, no church. Ethnicity alone leaves us separated from God and from each other. It is only through Jesus' sacrifice that we can become sons of God and can live within his blessing. It is only through Jesus' sacrifice that we can call each other brother.

After the Holy Spirit's blessing came to us at Shirati, other brethren from Kenya and Uganda, African members of the Anglican church, men who had earlier received God's blessing, came to visit us. It was like in the New Testament when Peter and John went to Samaria after hearing of the revival which was taking place through Philip's ministry. These brethren, whom the Holy Spirit had visited earlier, came to visit us. They gave witness that the Holy Spirit had truly come to us, opening our eyes, so we could see Jesus. They taught us more about how to walk together in the new way. They showed us that this was God's work among us and that all praise and glory for this awakening must go to him. These brethren bore witness about us to the brethren in Kenya and Uganda when they returned to their homes.

Because of the witness of these brethren, we became accepted as Cornelius was accepted through the witness of Peter to the other apostles in Jerusalem. We found then that everywhere in East Africa we were recognized as brothers of the same new village. It was wonderful to go to a place where you had never been before and to be welcomed as dear, honored relatives. An example of this new unity was that if a brother wished to marry but was so poor he didn't have the bride dowry, other brethren across ethnic and church boundaries would get the dowry together for him, just as they would were he their own blood brother.

This movement of God's Holy Spirit among the East African Christian denominations, a movement showing us Jesus' sacrifice as God's way into the new village, became known in the West as the East African Revival Fellowship. Here we know it simply as The Fellowship, *Ushirika.* It has never developed as a separate church but is present in all the churches throughout East Africa.

In some ways The Fellowship brings a division between people because it is not possible to accept a person as a brother in Jesus if this person has not publicly confessed his sin which separates him from God and from his brothers and accepted to be set free by the sacrificial blood of Jesus. If this has not happened, you can not fully entrust yourself to the other person.

In our own Mennonite church in those days there was only one bishop, Elam Stauffer. I accompanied him in his ministry all over the area of the Mennonite church. Revival covered all our churches from the Jita and Ruri peoples south of Musoma along the lake to the Zanaki and Kuria peoples in the highlands east of the lake. We all began to love and trust each other—missionaries, Bantu, and Nilotic together in the new village. We now had a framework for Africans to begin to assume responsible leadership, in the emerging Mennonite church, alongside the missionaries.

A youth choir

Bishop Kisare preaching at an open-air conference

Bishop and Susana Kisare

Leadership

Christian Ministry

A new hope was born in the hearts of the world's colonialized peoples at the close of World War II. Our new hope for freedom came with the opening of the United Nations Organization. Tanganyika was still a trust territory, and England continued to be our colonial administrator. But the United Nations promised that one day we would be freed.

In preparation for that day, the United Nations told England to develop an education system in the country. We bush school teachers were now required to have certificates. Because of this new government regulation, I got to go to school again.

The missionaries opened a small school at Shirati, teaching standards five and six. In 1946 and 1947 I was studying again. Missionary Vivian Eby was our teacher.

In the meantime Susana's and my family continued to grow. We were always hoping for a son. My village could not begin to grow until there were sons. During the years right after Bible school, when we were living near Susana's home at Rwang'enyi, our third daughter, Penina, was born. That was 1941.

The year of the Lord's blessing at Shirati, 1942, our third son was born. My heart was filled with joy. I named him David. But he also sickened and died, like his two older brothers before him, Joshua and Clement.

Following our one year at Shirati the church council assigned me to Nyahongo to open a bush school and shepherd a congregation. Nyahongo, like Rwang'enyi, is off the beaten track but it is nearer to the Shirati station, only

five miles away. Susana and I were happy at Nyahongo serving the Lord through 1945. While we were there our fourth
daughter, Stella, was born. During the two years 1946 and
1947, when I was back studying at Shirati, our fifth and
sixth daughters, Lois and Ruth, were born.

I didn't want to stop studying after finishing the sixth
standard. To be certified I needed teacher training, and I
couldn't begin that until I had finished standard eight. But
there was no opportunity for me to study beyond standard
six. So with two friends, Zefania Migire and Nikonor Dhaje, I
began private studies.

We got Samuel Ngoga's notebooks. He had gone across
the lake to the Katoke school near Bukoba and had finished
standard eight. We studied his standard seven and eight
notebooks. At that time students copied into their notebooks
each lesson which the teacher put on the blackboard. We
studied these notebooks in the evenings, without a teacher,
for two years.

When we felt we were ready, we went to Ikizu, some 100
miles away in South Mara, to take the government middle
school exam. I very nearly passed that exam. I was just a few
points below the pass line.

During the two years I was doing private study, I was
also teaching under a certified teacher in the Shirati
Primary School. This was an interim arrangement until
enough certified teachers could be trained. If I had passed
the Standard 8 exam, I would have been sent by the mission
for teacher training so I could be certified to teach. But I
didn't pass. So the door to teaching was closed to me. By this
time the missionaries had enough certified teachers for the
primary schools they were operating. I was no longer
employable.

I was now a man nearing 40 years of age. I couldn't start
building my life again. This was a very difficult time for me. It
was as though I had been fired. Teaching had been my life
from the time I graduated from the Bukiroba Bible School
ten years earlier. Even before that I had been helping John
Mosemann with teaching. This was my identity, teacher—
mwalimu. True, I had known that I didn't have enough
education to be a good teacher, but the very people who now

told me that I must stop teaching were the ones who earlier had refused to help me to get more education.

I knew they were embarrassed by this change in the weather, so to speak. They had not foreseen that the time would come when Africans also needed to be educated. Now there was nothing they could do. Even so, I felt betrayed.

Phebe Yoder was the education secretary for the Mennonite Mission. She knew my pain. She cried with me over this great rock which stood in my path. But she could do nothing to undo what had been done. I could no longer teach.

At that time the missionaries in South Mara were reaching out in evangelism beyond the boundaries of their church districts. One of the places they visited was some 60 miles up the Mara River from the lake, on the south side of the river, an area called Kisaka. This area was very sparsely settled by the Ngurimi people, Bantu hunters and cattle herders. It was an area bordering what is now the Serengeti National Park, a land with antelope and gazelle, and where lions roared at night.

Luo people from Kenya had been moving into this fertile river valley, farming it, and raising cattle. Among these settlers were Christians, formerly Anglicans, who welcomed the efforts of the Mennonite missionaries and pleaded with them to open a bush school and a place of regular worship. The settlers asked that a Luo teacher/evangelist be sent to live and work among them.

When I heard of this request, I knew in my heart that this is where I must go. To stay at Shirati would only nourish my confusion and bitterness. I knew that to harbor resentment against the missionaries was useless. There was nothing they could now do to make me a certified teacher. Something in my spirit told me that the way out of my darkness was to go to Kisaka. There God would give me light to see my path again.

Susana didn't want to go. By this time she had five or six close friends on the Shirati station, women her age, wives of church leaders and teachers. She had her fields where she raised our millet and cassava. In mid-1949 she gave birth to our seventh daughter, Tereza. The last thing she wanted to do was pull up her roots and move to Kisaka.

No road went to Kisaka. On the south side of the Mara River a road came to within fifteen miles and from there you could reach Kisaka with a vehicle, if you had one, by following cattle trails. From the north side of the river, a road went as far as a gold mine called Mara Mines. Then you could bushwhack by car through the high grass five miles to the river.

During the dry season one could wade the river. During the wet season one could cross by canoe, if the river remained within its banks. But when the valley flooded, there was no way to cross the river and the only way out of Kisaka was by walking west the 15 miles to the nearest road.

We left Shirati in September at the end of the dry season. Our two oldest daughters stayed behind with relatives. Susana wept that day as she bade farewell to her friends. James Shank drove us the 70 road miles to the crossing place on the north bank of the Mara River.

The Christians we were going to minister to met us there at the river and helped to carry our belongings across. Besides our sleeping mat and clothing, Susana had her cooking pots, dried fish, flour. I had brought a blackboard, the symbol of my profession, and a door for our house. After crossing the river, it was still a six-mile walk to our new home.

I had been to Kisaka before, with Elam Stauffer, on an evangelistic trip. The chief of the area had agreed that we might have one of the huts at what was called the Chief's Camp. This was where people would gather on occasion when there was government business to do.

There were some four or five huts at Chief's Camp unused except when the chief was there on business. He allowed us to use one of these huts, small, rectangular, one-room, grass-roofed, mud-and-stick-walled. It had no outside door, only a space in the wall for one. When we arrived, one of the men in the group welcomed us, and quickly put in the frame and hung the door which we had brought.

Then toward evening everyone went to his home, the nearest of which was a quarter mile away. Suddenly my wife and I with our five daughters were alone in a strange place with night coming on. There are mountains around Kisaka, and Susana felt hemmed in, imprisoned. She began to cry. I was unnerved myself. I assured her that if there were a bus we would leave at once for Shirati.

But there was no bus. We spread our sleeping mat; Susana got a cooking fire going for our evening meal. Someone had brought water from a nearby spring. Soon we fell into the rhythm of life in our new home. I set up my blackboard and began to teach.

My students were for the most part those several families from Kenya who had been Anglican, but were now Mennonite, who had called us to open a new work in that area. Some of them were married men; two were my age. These people restored my self-confidence. Life returned to my spirit. I was healed.

A few weeks after our arrival, the rains began and we found that Chief's Camp was situated in a swampy area. The dirt floor in our house was constantly wet. I built a rack of slats lashed to poles which we covered with grass to get the girls' sleeping mat up out of the wet. For Susana and me, I built a bed taking four forked posts, driving them into the floor for the four bedposts. On these posts I built a frame to which I lashed slats made from sisal poles, covered it with grass to take out the knots and spread our sleeping mat.

Surprisingly, very little meat was available and no fish. For our sauce to go with our *ugali* we used the leaves of a vine growing in that area. Since we were so far from communications lines, our Shs. 15/= ($2.50) monthly wage was often late and sometimes never reached us, having gotten lost on the way.

But the biggest problem was Susana's cooking fire. I tried to build up the driest corner of the house with earth to get her three-stone cooking place up out of the wet so her fire could burn hot enough to cook our daily *ugali*. Susana remembers crying one evening when her fire would only smoke. Nine-year old Penina comforted her, patting her side, saying, "Don't cry, Mother. God sees your work. He will remember you." She, our third daughter, is now a schoolteacher living with her family in Nairobi.

We lived at Kisaka only eight months. But during that time something else happened to me in addition to the restoration of my self-confidence as a teacher. There, far from home and from any other congregation, I saw that God was leading me into a full-time pastoral ministry. The classroom was taken from me; that path closed. But a new way was opening. Clearly I could now see this new path leading to Christian congregational ministry.

In June of 1950 we returned to Shirati for home leave. The river was high then at the end of the wet season. We crossed by canoe. Dr. Noah Mack met us with a vehicle on the north bank of the river.

We were not sure of our future and we had no one to leave our things with in the little house at Chief's Camp. So we took everything along with us. Our new brothers and sisters in Christ, seeing us tie up our few bundles, guessed that we wouldn't be back. Although they were sad to see us go, they gathered to wish us Godspeed. One of their number took up the leadership of the congregation.

It was harvest time when we came again to our people at Shirati. Many relatives and brethren in the church shared their harvests with us. In this way they made up our lack because we had been unable to plant our fields that year.

The Shirati District Church Council asked me to have oversight of the four congregations in the Rwang'enyi-Nyahongo area. I did this from Shirati, walking out for the weekend, my books in a basket on the end of my stick carried over my shoulder. I would go out on Saturday and return on Monday or Tuesday, visiting, leading worship, preaching, teaching catechism, building up the congregations.

We now had seven living children, all daughters. Of our three sons, Joshua had died shortly after birth. The next two, Clement and Daudi, had each lived for nearly a year. But they too had died.

After Daudi's death, Susana bore four more daughters. I despaired of ever having a son. Our income was very low, our home small; seven children were enough. I said to Susana, "You should be closed. It is enough, seven daughters. You are not strong. Every several years another daughter? No, it is not good. You should be closed." The missionary doctor would have done the operation closing her womb.

My wife, Susana, was alarmed. She looked up to see my

face, wondering if I were serious. Seeing that I was in earnest, she looked away in respect before replying, "Father of Margaret, there is yet within me another son. I may not be closed until I have borne you this son."

"Let us pray then," I said. "Let us pray to God that He may give to us this son of whom you speak."

We knelt there and then, together, committing our lives afresh to the one who had called us to this life together, one husband, one wife, covenanted exclusively each to the other until death. "*Nyasaye Nyakalaga*, hear our prayer; gift us with a son if it be in thy will for us."

In the rhythm of time Susana was again with child. On October 31, 1951, our son Abner was born. I gave him the second name *Mosi*, which in Swahili means "one"—Abner Mosi, only son of Marwa, son of Kisare.

My spirit told me that we would not again bear a son. In the following years Susana bore yet three more daughters, Phebe in 1954, Katerina in 1957, and Dorika in 1959. Thus, Susana bore to me in all four sons of whom one lives and ten daughters, 14 children, 11 living.

In July 1983, Margaret has 5 children, Miriam has 6, Penina has 6, Stella has 7, Lois has 4, Ruth has 4, Tereza has 5, Abner is unmarried, Phebe has 4, Katerina is unmarried, and Dorika has 1, for a total of 42 grandchildren. Susana and I have 7 great grandchildren. And that is not the end of them. They are still coming. But when I look at my village, it is still empty because Abner has not yet married. A village does not grow until there is a daughter-in-law.

Shortly after we returned from Kisaka in 1950, Bishop Stauffer came to Shirati from Mugango in South Mara where he was living. He came to Shirati for one of our District Church Council meetings. He told us, the elected church elders, that the church was growing and the work was now so great that the missionaries could not continue to do it alone.

In those days all the missionary men, even the doctors, were ordained pastors of the Mennonite church. Each church district was led by a missionary pastor who was chairman of the District Church Council. Each district had a number of congregations. The Shirati district at that time had about 10 congregations.

Bishop Stauffer told us that the time had come for Africans to be ordained. Bishop Stauffer had already discussed this proposal with the missionary pastors and they had agreed that the work was too great for them to carry without African help. The Shirati District Church Council discussed the issue and we also agreed that our bishop was right. We decided that two men should be chosen from Shirati. In South Mara two others would be chosen from the Mugango/ Majita church district.

Bishop Stauffer then told us that the two new pastors would be chosen by the Holy Spirit. This would be done by each church member speaking the name or names of one or two men as the Holy Spirit directed. The believers who had not yet been baptized would not bring names. Those who had been excommunicated from the church would not bring names. Only communicant members would speak a name or names. These names would be spoken in private to Bishop Stauffer and his missionary assistant.

Bishop Stauffer told us that if the Holy Spirit is leading the choice of African pastors, then only two names would be spoken by the church members. No ordination would take place until all the church members spoke the names of only two candidates. We elders in the church council agreed with Bishop Stauffer that this was the right way to go.

Bishop Stauffer then called a meeting of the whole district and announced to all the members what had been decided. He asked the members if they agreed that this was the right way to go. Everyone agreed.

To become a pastor seemed to everyone to be a very extraordinary thing. The only pastors we knew were the missionaries. They were our only role models. What we saw them doing was chairing the district council meetings, preaching and teaching. But we knew that African pastors would become part of the Pastors' Council, and they would eventually learn how the mission administration worked.

Many people desired this work. I was afraid because I could not see how our many factions at Shirati could agree on only two names. When people think in terms of their own villages, the task of leadership enters a great wilderness. I was afraid of this wilderness. Were only two names to be brought, then it would be like August 1942 when we all forgot our individual villages and saw only the new village of God.

This work was done in 1950. After several months of teaching in the congregations, the date was set to bring names.

At the first meeting to receive names more than two names were spoken. Most of the names given were for three men. So Bishop Stauffer told us to continue to pray and to seek the will of the Holy Spirit.

After several more months, he called for another meeting to receive names. This time only one person brought the name of the third man who had received many votes the first time. Bishop Stauffer called the man who had spoken the one name, and after he talked with him a long time, the man agreed to remove the name he had brought.

Bishop Stauffer then announced to the congregation that Zedekia Marwa Kisare and Nashon Kawira Nyambok had been unanimously chosen first African pastors in the Shirati District.

The congregation was filled with great grace. Spontaneously everyone began to sing "*Tukutendereza Yesu.*" This is a Ugandan language translation of the hymn which symbolized the East African Revival Fellowship. The congregation knew in their hearts that we were experiencing again our unity as members of the new village. They expressed this joy by singing in a Ugandan language.

Glory, glory hallelujah!
Praise be to the Lamb!
For the cleansing blood has reached me,
Hallelujah to the Lamb!

Soon the congregation had moved outside. The people were singing around the church. My old timidity returned. I was suddenly weak. So few from my village lived at Shirati. I was overwhelmed. How could I be a leader of these people?

My brother in Christ Nashon Nyambok came to me; he took my hand and he said, "Come, let us go outside to the people. Let us receive their joy."

That evening Bishop Stauffer came to my home to sit

with me, to talk, to give me encouragement, to welcome me
into the council of Mennonite pastors. That same evening
James Shank visited my brother Nashon Nyambok. It was
December 10, 1950.

Earlier that year two men from the Majita/Mugango
church district had been ordained, Ezekiel Kaneja Muganda
and Andrea Mawawa Mabeba. The four of us took a two-year
course in pastoral training at Bukiroba, 1951 and 1952.

Following those two years Pastor Nyambok expressed
his call to oversee the new work which was being opened in
the Tarime town. I accepted pastoral oversight for the Shirati
District.

I was the Shirati pastor until the end of 1958, a period
of six years. After that I moved into another kind of
leadership—teaching in the Bukiroba Bible School. Looking
back now, I remember those years I was pastoring as good
years. If your life is guided by a few important principles, pastoring isn't difficult.

It is most important that a leader in the church be filled
with the Holy Spirit so that as he studies the Scriptures he
may have revealed to him the true intent of the passage. A
leader needs to love the Scriptures. He must allow his life to
be led by God's Word. Every time a new translation of the Bible comes out, I buy it, in order to see how my favorite
passages have been worded.

Recently I was in Dar es Salaam and saw the *Jerusalem
Bible* for the first time. I bought it. When I got home Susana
asked me, "Are you going to fill our food pantry with books?"
She had a point because she manages our budget. But she
does not see how important it is to me to understand the
message in the Word.

What a leader teaches and preaches must grow out of
his inner character. We experience people in layers. First we
see only the outer layer of a person; first impressions are
formed by that outer layer. Integrity means that as we come
to know a person better and better, as we get to know his inner layers, we discover consistency. What a leader shows to
the public, what he shows in the pulpit, must have consistency with his innermost personality.

There is a Bantu saying that a person is like a thicket.

You do not know what is in a thicket. If you throw a rock into a thicket, you don't know what will come out. Maybe a rabbit will come hopping out or maybe a lion will leap out, roaring, intending to kill you. A thicket hides what it contains.

But with a Christian leader it must not be so. What is seen on the outside must be a true reflection of what is there on the inside. This is especially important for a leader's family. A man's wife and children know his inner life. If there is a split between his public and private life, he creates a great wilderness for his family.

A leader cannot force righteousness on people by angry shouting and heated argument. His leadership can quickly become like that of the Pharisees, a set of rules, the proper way to do things. Then, if people do not follow the right way, he harangues them, trying to beat them into line. He only makes people hard this way. Their hearts become closed to him. Even in his private life a leader should not be quarrelsome, peevishly picking at everything. Being this way only shows his own unsettledness.

A leader should not be a joker or back slapper. He loses his power and grace if the level at which he communicates with people is the exchange of witticisms. A leader should have a good sense of humor and should joy in life's pleasures. He should laugh and should be able to encourage others to laugh too. But it isn't good to be tricky and clever. A leader's speech should be full of wisdom and sound judgment. He should be gentle in manner and his behavior should be orderly.

Leaders must avoid gossip, *masengenyo*. A leader knows many things about his congregation. He knows about his fellow pastors. Sometimes a leader will talk with his friends or relatives about the things he knows concerning other people. Any such talk that is intended to undermine another person or to diminish his/her reputation is wrong. When a leader talks like this to others, all he is doing is showing his own nakedness. By gossiping he loses the trust of the people and he opens himself to attack by his enemies.

In order to stand firmly against evil in society, a leader needs to be seen by the people to be in a right relationship with God. His relationship to God cloaks him, as a garment covers the naked, giving him power to speak the truth. His relationship to God gives him power so people don't take his leadership jokingly. People are afraid to take him lightly or to brush his teaching aside.

He carries with him a certain moral power, even when his words are few, which brings others to see their hypocrisies and selfishness so they may repent and find forgiveness and cleansing through Jesus' sacrifice. Even if they don't repent, they are afraid to tangle with him.

But if a leader is gossiping to others, then his garment of right-standing with God is stripped off him and he is defenseless prey to any who choose to attack him. His ministry is powerless.

A wrestler has power as long as his two feet are firmly on the ground. Here in Africa you conquer your wrestling opponent by tripping him so he falls. A gossiping leader is like a wrestler with only one leg. His opponent may pick him up any way he likes and toss him where he pleases.

It is good for a leader to cultivate the presence of God's grace in his life, a serenity born of the presence of the Holy Spirit. When I am in harmony with God, it is as though I am in an ocean of peace and joy. This serenity gives power to my witness in the world. It opens my life to God's activity on my behalf because I am within the stream of God's active will on earth.

This serenity is sometimes broken. Maybe my wife comes suddenly, breaking into my thoughts of God, reminding me of some problem or issue which needs my attention. Maybe the children come shouting through the house, slamming the doors. Maybe someone comes with a complex bit of administration which he is pushing me to quickly decide on or do something about. Then I answer roughly in frustration. I lash out angrily at my detractors. It is then that the vase of grace slips from my hands, shattering on the floor.

When this happens, a light goes out in my soul. That grace of God's presence cannot be recovered without great effort and cost. I can't just pick it up again and be at peace. No. Recovery requires repentance and cleansing and a return to that attitude of mind which again welcomes God's presence. What I should do is to respond to the daily barrage of detractions with equanimity, in a spirit of grace. Then the day's work and activity go forward blessed always by God's presence.

Too often a leader is like a small child who takes a pencil and, not knowing the proper use of it breaks it; or he is like a child who, not knowing the function of a knife, cuts himself. When a leader treats God's grace lightly and goes about his activity roughly behaving like those who don't know God, it shows that he is immature in his understanding of grace. Grace then turns again to harm him and he is empty, forspent. God's intent in gifting us with grace is to empower us so we may face each issue and task with confidence in peace.

When it has been my duty to confront another person, maybe even a pastor in the church, I take Galatians 6:1-2 as my guide. "Brothers, if someone is caught in a sin, you who are spiritual should restore him gently. But watch yourself, or you also may be tempted. Carry each other's burdens, and in this way you will fulfill the law of Christ." I cannot help someone, if I have disdain in my heart for him. If I despise someone, then all I do when visiting him is to trade insults. No good comes of it.

Once, after I became a bishop, I needed to go to a pastor about sin in his life. He was not from my tribe. I was very afraid to go to him because he could take my coming to him ethnically. He might think I was picking on him. But more than this, I feared to go because he was my age-mate. As human beings we were equal.

I took with me another pastor, a brother with whom I had peace, a man of wisdom and grace. We went then, after much prayer, in a spirit of humility and gentleness. We did not go to him like holy people, but like fellow pilgrims. He received us with great fear. I asked myself, "Who am I that I should come to this man with this word?" I honored him in how I approached him, and he in turn honored me in how he received my word.

Almost always if a youth in the church sees the mistake of his elder, the youth will be afraid to speak to his elder. Usually the youth will do nothing. But it need not be so. The main thing is for the youth to be free. If a person is free, he can speak the truth. The youth is free if he wishes for honor and goodwill to be given to his elder. Sometimes the youth may wish to cut down the older person, to neutralize him. Then going to the elder only creates a quarrel. But if the youth is free, then the elder can receive help from the youth. This happens between me and my children. They are free and they approach me with their insights and counsel.

Sometimes there is something a leader feels strongly about, some work or project which he wishes to see move forward, but others do not see it that way. Other people can prevent the leader's vision from taking place.

There are two ways to look at such a situation. One is to follow good administrative common sense. There are reasons why the leader's vision has not been accepted. It is not good for the leader just to forget about his idea if it was not accepted the first time. It is good to talk about the idea freely with those people who are involved so that his idea is understood and its various possibilities become clear. Certainly if it is a good idea, then in due course there will be agreement on the best way to put it to work.

But it may be possible that the leader's vision was misguided, or maybe his plan was good but the circumstances changed so that his plan is no longer appropriate. A leader should always keep an open mind so that he is not bitter if it is not possible to do what he had wanted to do.

The Fellowship brothers and sisters use the idea of brokenness, *kuvunjika*. When a leader is broken, he accepts the collective wisdom of the group, he accepts a situation different from what he had himself wanted. The insight of the Fellowship brethren is that if a leader is broken to his own way, then God opens up for him a new and better way. "Be broken to this," they say, "and God will make it up to you. He will give you something better."

To refuse to be broken is just to live in bitterness in the past. A leader living in bitterness never grows. His spirit remains stunted, his leadership sterile. Brokenness, as the Fellowship understands it, sets the leader free and sets God free. It brings a resurrection power into his experience, something new is born out of the ashes of that which failed.

A leader should be close to young people. Youth are

strong and brave. They are full of hope, always looking outward, discovering the world and its possibilities. The leader, often an older person, has much experience, and he can give words of wisdom to the youth. The young and the old need to walk together if the church is to grow and be strong.

I love music. Choirs are my delight. I try always to promote choirs. In our spiritual life conferences I give the young people a large part of the program for their choirs. Sunday worship is too dull if there is no choir to brighten the service. We all need each other in the church, each contributing his or her part according to the gifts and station which each has.

A Wider Ministry— Interchurch Leadership

During my early years in Christian ministry I could never make ends meet. Poverty was always our companion. From time to time Bishop Stauffer helped me with gifts of money so I could get out of debt for a while. He was a caring brother to me. Once I remember he gave me a coat. On several occasions he helped me with money so I could begin a retailing business.

For a while I sold fish. At another time I sold bicycles. But I don't have the gift of selling things. Even Susana said people would buy from me only because they took pity on me. I am not a businessman. Using money to make money is a skill I do not have. All these ventures collapsed.

My father was a craftsman who made shields and spears. Many of his sons and grandsons have inherited skillful hands. But I am not skillful with my hands. I even have trouble with so simple a thing as fixing a flat bicycle tire. Bishop Stauffer would laugh when he saw me working to get the tire off the rim, and he would help me. The area in which I could have excelled, teaching, required more training than I was able to get. So Susana and I lived on my tiny church-work stipend and on the food she raised in her fields.

In 1954 Donald R. Jacobs arrived as a new missionary to work with us here in Tanzania. He was a forward-looking person and things began to change. I do not fully understand

how the change came about. But with the arrival of Don
Jacobs, our situation began to improve.

He knew his own aspirations in life and he was not
upset to see us wishing to wear leather shoes and have cement floors in our houses. He was well educated and it didn't
offend him that we loved learning too. He did everything he
could to help us to rise above our low economic and in-
tellectual state. His greatest gift to us was that he saw us as
brothers and sisters on equal standing with him. He saw us
as fellow human beings on the same level.

Don Jacobs wasn't just an intelligent person. Solving
people's problems only with intelligence gets us nowhere. For
change to happen, change that is good, Jesus must be at the
center of that change. Soon after Jacobs came to Tanganyika
he met Jesus in the same way that we had met him, along
with Bishop Stauffer, back in 1942.

So from near the beginning of Don's experience as a
missionary, his work and his estimation of us was based not
only on his good education and his bright intelligence but on
the blood of Jesus which breaks down the walls which
separate people from each other. In this way Don Jacobs, like
Bishop Stauffer before him, was our brother at the foot of the
cross.

At the Bible school there were no African teachers. Of
course none of us was educated enough to teach there.
Besides, the purpose of the Bible school was to teach us
about how the church in the West understood and practiced
Christianity so there was no reason to have African teachers.

Don Jacobs became the principal of the Bible school. He
persuaded the missionaries and Elam Stauffer that it was
not good to continue without any African teachers. An African teacher could help the students to connect what they
were learning with their African background. This was a new
idea, a Jacobs' kind of idea. I was chosen to be the African
teacher. We moved to Bukiroba in 1959. Little did we realize
that this central Mennonite station would be our home for
the next 21 years.

I was delighted to get back to teaching. Not only did I
enjoy my work, but I also got a bit higher salary than I was
getting as a pastor. At first we were given a student's house,

three small rooms connected by a small dining area. To me this seemed to say that I wasn't really a teacher. But John Leatherman added a room to a house nearby and put in ceiling board. When we moved into this larger house, our living situation showed that my status as teacher was being taken seriously.

Susana as "the teacher's wife" was an elder sister and mother to the students' wives. Sharing with them and encouraging them out of her own experience, she helped many of them to mature in their lives in the church. These women came from many different tribes. Susana was blind to tribal differences. She related to everyone in the same way. This was her gift—affirming and encouraging people.

I taught the Gospel of Matthew, Evangelism, English, and Arithmetic. I knew a little English because over the years I had been doing private studies in this language. Dorothy Smoker gave me a simple English textbook to use with the students. I think the main idea the missionaries had in teaching English in the Bible school was not that they thought the students should learn English. Rather, it was a way to quiet the persistent begging of students to be taught this language. I taught such simple things as "that, those, this, and these." I do not think that through these simple efforts my students learned much useful English.

The Gospel of Matthew was a joy to teach. I like the way Matthew shows that Jesus was the Savior who was foretold by the Old Testament prophets, how his sacrifice on the cross was foreshadowed by the Old Testament sacrifices. The Transfiguration, which is recorded by Matthew, shows this link between Jesus and the Old Testament.

The resurrection always fills me with a special delight. People are so blind and stupid. They planned to bury God without stopping to consider whether God could be buried. The authorities put guards to watch so God would stay in his grave. The soldiers, seeing nothing unusual about their assignment, fell asleep. Early Easter morning Jesus came calmly walking out of the grave. When reality finally broke through to the guards, they were utterly dumbstruck, falling about as though struck dead. Thus it always is to those who in their stupidity think small thoughts about God. I would so much love to have been watching when the guards awoke and saw Jesus coming out of the grave!

Teaching evangelism was my greatest joy. This course had a lot of practical work connected with it. Not only was evangelism an important course in the school, it was the core purpose of the school. The school existed to help church leaders in their work as evangelists and shepherds of the believers. All the teachers held this to be the important thing. Even the missionaries who weren't teachers saw this as the reason for the existence of the Bible school.

In my role as teacher of evangelism, I spent many weekends with students visiting villages in various areas where the church was still new. Usually the missionaries provided transport and we traveled up to 100 miles away, reaching as far as Robanda, Ikoma, at the edge of the Serengeti National Park.

Looking back now on those years, I praise the missionaries for putting the emphasis at the right place. But I think the emphasis on evangelism would have been strengthened if they would have more seriously worked at teaching English and administration. The main skill we teachers developed in the students was preaching. Building up the church requires skills and gifts in addition to preaching.

In 1960 freedom was in the air. The United Nations was pushing England to give us our independence. People began to think in radically different ways. The church too would become independent. Africans would become responsible to administer the church's programs. There was even talk of an African bishop. These were new and exciting ideas. They were also sober ideas because the future was upon us, and no one had been getting ready for the future.

In 1961 Don Jacobs returned to Africa from two years of study in America. He was now Dr. Jacobs. Right away he began plans to help us older pastors catch up, so to speak. The missionaries saw that they had held us back so they now worked to make some of that up to us.

A theological college was built at Bukiroba. In 1963 the Bible school was closed for a while and the theological college was opened. This was a school for pastors. The missionaries wanted to gift us with this school before they left. I, along with 15 other men, began a three-year course.

Two things happened to me during those three years. First, I studied English seriously for the first time in my life. Soon I was reading the language fairly well, especially the English Scriptures. I also got so that I could follow English preaching and teaching. I was able to follow an English conversation. But my spoken English remained broken and I am still embarrassed to use it. I think that, if I had had a fourth year of English study, I would have begun to use it comfortably in conversation.

The second thing that happened during those three years was that I discovered my traditional theological roots. Up to this time the missionary approach to our African heritage was to say that it was all savagedom, *ushenzi*. There was no effort to connect the gospel message to our traditional faith.

It wasn't only the Mennonite missionaries who swept all of that aside. Very few missionaries of any other denomination looked seriously at Africa's traditional faith. This was part of the colonial mind-set about Africa.

Trustingly, we accepted the missionaries' assessment of our traditional beliefs, and we actually thought that as Christians we had cleansed ourselves of all traditional influences. Don Jacobs changed all this for us, his 16 students. He taught the theology courses.

The first year he taught us African Traditional Theology. At first we were amazed that he knew about these things. This was a subject that had never been discussed with the missionaries except in terms of rejecting it. Now Jacobs taught it as though he himself were an African traditionalist. We found that Jacobs understood us. He helped us to understand ourselves.

We saw that our traditional world view was there in our subconscious, influencing us in ways we had never seen before. For the first time I became aware of the reality of spiritual power. I saw how satanic power works secretly and in darkness to bring chaos and disruption into a society. I came to understand the traditional answers to the problem of evil. I came to see the traditional role of the family in salva-

tion and life after death. Often, as Don walked out the door at
the close of his teaching period, the whole class would erupt
in excited talk as we shared with each other the new dis-
coveries we were making.

The second and third years Jacobs taught us Christian
theology through the perspective we had gotten the first
year. We saw the answers Christian faith brings to life's
issues. We saw these answers in the light of the answers
traditional faith brings. We began to see where the Christian
faith is in conflict with the traditional faith, and we saw the
places where Christian faith is the complement or fulfillment
of traditional faith.

The first year I had become especially aware of how the
traditional faith manipulates spiritual power. Now I saw how
the power of Jesus' sacrifice neutralizes Satan's power, setting us free from its debilitating influence. Again time after
time the class would erupt in excited talk at the close of the
teaching period as we processed together what we were
learning.

Through these classes I came to put all ethnic religion
on one level, whether it be Nilotic, Bantu, Swiss-German, or
Jewish—the lot of them are only guides to life in terms of the
insights of people's ancestors. All of them tie people up in
ethnic regulations which are a barrier to the discovery of
freedom in Jesus.

Salvation is not found in ethnic religion, although
ethnic religion may point the way to salvation. Salvation is
found only through the blood sacrifice Jesus made on the
cross. This same saving blood pushes over the ethnic walls
which separate one people from another. Jesus' sacrifice
provides the linkage which makes all peoples one new people.

During the third year of the theological college I pur-
posed in my heart to resign from official church leadership.
My heart was full of the message of salvation. I saw so clearly
how our traditional Luo way of life finds its fulfillment in
Jesus. I decided to return to Shirati and give the rest of my
life to itinerant preaching. I would support myself as a cattle
herdsman.

In East African schools a final exam is given at the end
of a course of study. The day for the final exam was set. When

we entered the classroom, we found that Dorothy Smoker had written the examination on the blackboard. Instead of giving us paper on which to write our answers she called on me to come to the front of the class and asked me to orally answer the questions. This I did, along with answering additional questions which she asked in order to clarify what I had already said.

At the end of the exam she announced that the theological college teachers had chosen me to be the principal of the Bible school when it reopened! I was dumbfounded. But deep in my heart there was a responding "Yes" to this call. In a few months when the Bible school reopened I had for my staff Pastor Salmon Buteng'i and Caleb Randa, both graduates with me in the theological college class of '65.

Salvation is so easy to understand, so difficult to practice. From the beginning, the Mennonite Church in Tanganyika (changed to Tanzania in 1964) has had two main tribal groups in it. To the north there are the Luo, a Nilotic people. To the south there are the Jita/Ruri, Bantu peoples. In the early 1960s these two groups made up two thirds of the church membership. The rest of the members were mostly Kuria and Zanaki—also Bantu peoples. There were also some Ngurimi and Ikoma Mennonites—also Bantu.

Most of these groups by the early 1960s had pastors and deacons. How could these many peoples agree together on who should be their bishop? The church constitution said that a bishop is to be chosen by a 75 percent majority vote of all the pastors and deacons.

During the time I was a teacher in the Bible school, before the theological college was opened, Bishop Stauffer called a meeting to choose the first African bishop. The meeting was at Bumangi.

That meeting was a difficult and unhappy experience. The pastors gave two names, Ezekiel Muganda's and mine. He was from Majita, and I was from Shirati. We voted several times but neither Ezekiel nor I got the 75 percent majority needed. So Bishop Stauffer announced that at that time it was not possible to choose an African bishop.

Many young church leaders and school teachers had

come to Bumangi to celebrate the choosing of an African bishop. When neither of us could get 75 percent of the vote, they called a meeting which became noisy. Many unpleasant things were said.

Ezekiel and I hated such a meeting where God's work became political. Many of the young church leaders and teachers were saying that we should have two African bishops since neither of us had gotten 75 percent. But others warned us not to do this. As brothers together in one church it was necessary that we wait until it became clear which one person should be our first bishop.

At a later meeting, the pastors and deacons unanimously asked Don Jacobs to be our bishop until it would be clear who the first African bishop should be. We made this decision because the two missionary bishops, Elam Stauffer and Simeon Hurst, were retiring from missionary work. Bishop Jacobs also planned to leave Tanzania. After the graduation of the first class in the theological college, the mission board at Salunga wanted him to move to Nairobi. In 1965 Bishop Jacobs announced that again it was time to choose an African bishop.

I was concerned when Don made this announcement because I knew that the two candidates would be the same two people as the first time. I remembered Bumangi. I do not like these meetings where people strive against each other. I remembered the struggle we had at Shirati when Pastor Nashon Nyambok and I were finally chosen to be the first pastors there. I wanted to go far away and leave all these struggles to other people.

I prayed for wisdom to know what to do. This situation was so difficult for me that I decided to go to Kenya to ask the brethren in the Revival Fellowship for counsel. They were not Mennonites so they would not have a vested interest in giving me advice about what to do.

I went first to Nairobi to the Fellowship brethren there. I asked them for counsel on two matters. Should I accept to go through with whatever wrangling might take place during the selection process? My second question was whether I ought in any case to accept to become a bishop should the vote fall on me. I felt that such high office could turn me away from my simple faith so that I might lose sight of Jesus and become just a worldly leader.

The brethren with one voice gave me two answers. First they said that I was being timid about the selection process. They told me that Jesus does not give us "a spirit of timidity, but a spirit of power, of love and of self-discipline" (2 Timothy 1:7). They gave me courage with these words.

In their second answer they reminded me that there was a struggle all over East Africa in the churches between pastors and bishops over the Revival Fellowship. Many pastors and bishops were not sympathetic to the Fellowship and worked against it. They showed me that the life of any bishop in East Africa who was a brother in the Fellowship would be a testimony to the other bishops of God's saving power, even in high office. The bishops get together, especially in the National Christian Councils, and there a saved brother would be a testimony to the other bishops. They assured me that high office does not cause a person to lose Jesus.

Next I went to Kisumu. The brethren there told me the same things the brethren in Nairobi had told me. They said that even the missionaries had not been able to bring peace and love between church leaders. Only Jesus can do that. So if a brother who is being saved by Jesus is called by his church to high office, he should accept it.

After meeting with these brethren I was at peace. My fear was gone. Bishop Jacobs called a meeting of all the pastors and deacons at Bukiroba in February 1966. At the first vote both Ezekiel Muganda and I were named, but neither of us got 75 percent. By this time we were both graduates of the theological college. At the second vote I had almost all the votes.

Bishop Jacobs dismissed the meeting to enable us to go and rest a bit. He then called us together again for a prayer service. Many of my fellow pastors prayed, giving thanks to God for having brought us to this day. They prayed for me that I would have strength and courage for the work which lay ahead.

Although I took up my bishop responsibilities right away, it was decided that my ordination would be the following year, January 1967. We invited Bishop Elam Stauffer to

come along with Bishops David Thomas and Donald Lauver
from the United States. We invited the bishops of the
Catholic, Anglican, and Lutheran churches in Mara Region.
The Fellowship brethren from Kenya came. Of course, all the
Mennonite pastors and deacons came along with many,
many people. The ordination was held at Bukiroba, the
central station. It was planned to have only one service in the
morning followed by the noon meal so people would not need
to stay overnight in Bukiroba.

Bishop Lauver preached the sermon. I remember clearly
his illustration of a ship. He said that Christian ministry is
like a great ship on the ocean coming to people who are crying out in their need. The ship is full of cargo, the treasures
of God, which the minister is bringing to those people who
accept God's salvation. He said that this is the work of
ministry in the church to take the message of salvation to
the people so they may receive God's blessings.

Bishop Thomas then called me forward to take the
charge. After I answered his questions saying, "Yes," he
asked me to kneel, and he began to tell me what is required of
a bishop. He told me to be open to people, not harsh in
leadership. He said that it will be my responsibility to guard
the purity of the church in receiving members and in excom-
municating those who have fallen away from the faith.

Bishop Thomas then welcomed me as a fellow bishop in
the Mennonite Church.

After the service Bishop Kibira—the Lutheran representative—and Arch Deacon Nyaronga—the Anglican representative—both brothers in the Revival Fellowship, announced to the congregation that they would take me to my
house while singing praises to Jesus.

My house was close to the church. It was the house
where Don Jacobs used to live. A procession went singing
with us to the house. Later a meal was served under the trees
near my house where a large *banda* or shelter had been
built. A bull had been butchered and there was rice and *ugali*
in abundance. We also had European bread and tea and soft
drinks for everyone. Everyone ate and was satisfied.

Pastor Ezekiel Muganda, who is now gone, was my
brother in Jesus. Before I was ordained bishop, he was the

pastor of the Musoma town church. I regarded him as having been a great man of God. I still regard him so. It is true that he had hoped to be the bishop. But when he saw that this did not happen, he determined to support me in every way. His support was very important to me because he was the senior Jita pastor.

Just one example of his acceptance of my leadership is this refrigerator here in my home. Shortly after I was ordained bishop a refrigerator became available from the mission. Many people wanted it. But Pastor Muganda used a Bantu proverb saying, "Not everyone can grow a beard; let our leader have the refrigerator."

Few of us have hair on the face. Often an African is quite old before he can grow a beard. So we have this saying meaning that if leadership has fallen on someone the rest should not quarrel with that. Pastor Muganda's wanting me to have the refrigerator showed that he accepted my position as bishop.

The heartland of the Jita-Ruri people is down in Majita, Pastor Muganda's homeland, 35 miles south of Musoma along the lake. The Majita A Church District has its central church at Mrangi. Pastor Aristarko Masese is the leader of this district. For a long time Majita A has been one of the largest districts in terms of numbers of congregations and a large church membership. I loved to go to Mrangi. Pastor Masese always showed me great hospitality. Whenever church guests came from overseas, I would take them to Mrangi. Every year I delighted in going to the Mijita A annual spiritual life conference.

No other church district showed me as much respect as was shown me by the Majita A District. In 1967 church secretary Eliam Mauma and I went to Amsterdam for Mennonite World Conference. When we returned, Pastor Masese invited us to Mrangi to celebrate our safe trip. They gave me a young bull to take home with me. They gave Mauma a heifer. Such a display of love I have never experienced before or since. The love and hospitality of the Jita people were especially precious to me because they were Pastor Ezekiel Muganda's people.

Pastor Muganda and I worked together in North and

South Mara preaching the gospel. A number of times he went to Kenya with me for spiritual life conferences among our young churches there. When the Lord took him home in 1974, I lost a dear and faithful brother who by his life showed to everyone the unity between people of different backgrounds which may be experienced because of Jesus' sacrifice.

I had bishop oversight of the whole church for 14 years. During that time the church expanded across the border into Kenya, where there were three church districts. In Tanzania there were Mennonite congregations in Mwanza, Biharlanulo, Tabora, Arusha and Dar es Salaam, in addition to the 13 church districts in Mara Region.

In 1979 a second bishop was ordained, Bishop Hezekia Nyamuko Sarya. After his ordination most of the pastors and deacons wanted to form two dioceses with the Mara River as the boundary. So the church is now two independent dioceses. I moved back to Shirati, where I assumed responsibility for the North Mara Diocese and for the Kenya Mennonite Church. Bishop Sarya was pastoring the congregation in Dar es Salaam when he was ordained. He moved to Bukiroba, where he assumed responsibility for the South Mara Diocese and the scattered congregations in other areas of Tanzania.

During the 21 years Susana and I lived at Bukiroba, my creative energies were consumed by the work of the church. At the end of my tenure at Bukiroba, I realized that I had quite neglected my physical base at Shirati. Back in the 1950s, when I was the pastor at Shirati, I had built a mud-brick house with a corrugated iron roof. From the outside the house looks a bit like the first missionary house which I helped build in 1934. But while at Bukiroba I neglected personal things; I planted no trees on my land; I let the house fall into disrepair.

When the time came for us to return to Shirati in 1979, I was crying because there was nothing at Shirati for me to go home to. A brother gave me courage saying that someone had to give his energies to the church. If no one was found to give of himself to the church, how could the message of salvation spread, how could the body of Christ be built up? This brother told me that God had called me to give my life to the church so I should not regret having no trees on my plot at Shirati. The God who called me to this ministry will be my God even in my old age. He will always be with me. So now looking back I do not regret those many years given to the church.

When Susana and I moved back to Shirati, we were warmly welcomed. The Shirati people provided a church house for us on the station. They slaughtered a bull and had a feast in our honor. Many people brought us grain and cassava so that we had a sufficient store of food to last more than a year. Since returning to Shirati, I have begun to build my house on the plot next to the mud brick one I built so long ago. I have planted trees, scores of them, on my piece of land. Some of the trees are now taller than I am.

My greatest fulfillment as bishop hasn't been in administration. My greatest joy has always been in seeing men and women come into a right relationship with God. I am always looking and praying for God's breaking into our congregations through the Holy Spirit bringing men and women into a right relationship with each other and with God. This is why I never tire being on the road, spending endless numbers of weekends visiting the churches, preaching and teaching the Word.

I praise the Lord that Susana has always worked with me in this ministry right up to today. She always goes along on my trips, packing up on Friday and spending the weekend in a tent or spare bedroom somewhere, always quietly at my side, returning home again on Sunday afternoon to her household responsibilities. When we travel she always has her seat in the front of the LandRover next to the door opposite the driver.

Through the years as a church leader I have learned that it is important to live life joyfully and creatively. My greatest recreation is visiting the churches, preaching salvation through Jesus' sacrifice and delighting in seeing people freed from the bondage of sin. But I enjoy physical things too. If I were younger, I think I would begin jogging. I like to see the young missionaries jogging.

I walk for exercise. I like to go out early in the morning

when the day is waking up. I go to the church to pray or I just walk around the block. When I walk, I take my knobkerrie, which is a carry-over from my youth when I herded my father's cattle. If I walk with my hand empty, I feel awkward. I think people seeing me must see my walk as unbalanced. I guess it is like a jogger wearing street shoes. He is embarrassed to jog without jogging shoes. I am embarrassed to walk without my stick.

I do not like old or secondhand things. These in the West are called antiques. I do not like antiques. I like new things and I like variety, new styles, new songs, new cups for tea, new shoes. I love to travel to see new places and to discover how people in different cultures do things.

Travel has spoiled me. I can no longer be content living under a thatched roof in a mud hut. I am not happy without light at night and without water on tap. But I am like my father in not liking to live in the midst of many people. Many people mean less peace and quiet.

I would like to retire and live at Kirongwe, enjoying the cool evening breezes off the lake which I enjoyed in my childhood. But there is no running water or electricity at Kirongwe so I will never retire there.

I get great joy from animals. Any animal which is an excellent specimen of its breed fills me with delight. I especially delight in wild animals. My great joy is visiting the Serengeti and seeing God's herds of animals there.

Every year I go hunting. I go with Zedekia Siso or with Glen Brubaker who both have high powered rifles. I have an Italian Breda 12-gauge shotgun which I take along. I buy the license but I let them do the shooting. It isn't the shooting that I enjoy so much. It is seeing the animals. We shoot a few for meat to help pay for the trip.

I spend time each day reading the Word. Every morning I read the daily meditation in English from *Living Light.* Whenever there are phrases I do not understand, I look them up in other English translations, or I check them in the two Swahili translations I have. I do not use a concordance. I know the Bible well enough so that I can find any passage after a moment of reflection on where it is. I love to prepare sermons, working at them thematically, fitting the message to the local frames of reference.

I enjoy the late afternoons when I get one of my grand-children to take several chairs outside to the back of the house. There I sit and visit with anyone who passes. That is a good time to drop by to greet me, when the day is cool at about 5:00 p.m.

Washing hands before a meal

Healing

Shortly after I was chosen in 1966 to be the first African bishop, I began to have a serious health problem. You remember that I was living at Bukiroba, the central station, at that time. My blood pressure was high. From time to time I had sudden attacks when I experienced pain and great pressure in my chest. At such a time I was unable to breathe. These attacks would last for several hours. During these attacks each time I expected to die.

The missionary doctors also thought that I would die during one of the attacks. I found out later that they had even reported on my condition to the mission board at Salunga, telling them that because of the high blood pressure I was not expected to live very long.

My first serious attack came in 1967 when I was on an administrative trip to the Shirati district. We went on a joint hospital-church trip to Burere, 18 miles from Shirati. We hoped the peasant farmers there would agree to give us a plot of land for a church. I expected the meeting with the Burere people the next day to be a difficult one.

That night I was in Dr. Glen Brubaker's tent. The attack came on me in my sleep. Hearing my distress, Glen awoke. He was alarmed at my condition. He got me some medicine, but he didn't have the right kind along. I went outside because I could not catch my breath in the closeness of the tent.

I went over to a nearby house where a number of the church elders were sleeping. They spread a mat on the floor and had me lie down. The pressure only got worse. Sit up, lie down, on my back, on my side—nothing helped. I assumed

115

that death was near.

That year in the Burere area eighteen people were killed by leopards. My need for air was so great that the thought of leopards never entered my mind. I felt no fear of anything, just this terrible grip on my chest. I sat in the open doorway, alone. The others went back to sleep.

Finally the lake breeze picked up, as it usually does around midnight. This cooler air slowly, slowly, eased the pressure. After some time I got up very carefully—like a wounded animal that is crawling away to die. I crept quietly to Glen's tent and lay down very gently on my bed hoping that the pressure would not grip me again. Then I slept.

The next day I was all right. The meeting was a difficult one, as I had anticipated. There was a big fuss, *ugomvi*, but eventually the question was settled without bitterness. During that whole meeting I was all right.

About a year after the experience at Burere, I was again on an administrative trip to Shirati. That night I was in one room of the Shirati guesthouse; my driver, Magoma, was in the other. Suddenly, in the middle of the night, my illness returned. I went outside and stood against the car trying somehow to get coolness from its metal. As before, nothing helped. I was in great pain, suffocating.

Magoma awakened and I sent him to get the doctor. It seemed the doctor would never come. At last, with the first rooster crowing, he came. He brought with him two syringes. It seemed to me that he pulled the pressure out of me with the needle. Miraculously, I could breathe again.

The doctors gave me some medications to help keep the symptoms of my illness in check. But I could feel the sickness there inside waiting to leap up in a moment, crushing out my life.

In 1972 I had another frightening attack. I had gone to Jita land for the annual weekend spiritual life conference of the Majita B church district. The conference was held in the town of Bunda. Nearly a thousand people had gathered from twenty Jita congregations.

On Saturday after the evening meal, we had a youth rally in the street outside Pastor Daniel Mato's house, where I was staying. The rally lasted until after 10:00 that night.

Pastor Mato's wife had prepared hot water for me to bathe following the rally.

I think it was the steam from the water in the small bathing cubicle which triggered the attack this time. It was my worst attack. There was no doctor and I had no medicine. My wife was called. We sat together outside the house trying to catch some cool night air. Susana held my hand.

Pastor Mato went to find a man called Adonias, who ran a little Mennonite bookshop in the town. Adonias also sold medicines. Pastor Mato hoped that Adonias might have even one pill of the medicine I needed. Adonias had two of these pills. By 2:00 a.m. the pressure had let up. When I got release I was still frightened that the pressure would leap suddenly upon me again. So I went very slowly and gently to my place of sleep.

The next day was the last day of the conference. Many people had come for this Sunday morning meeting. My wife refused to let me preach. Pastor Mato was in distress knowing that everyone was expecting that I would bring one of the messages that morning. I saw that if I did not preach then, the word would spread everywhere that I had been struck down with sudden illness. I saw that it would not be good for the church if all these people went home to their houses scattered across Jita land reporting that I was incapacitated. God gave me courage and I decided to preach. God gave me strength. I was able to preach in my normal way.

I felt now within myself that my condition was not good. One of these times I would die.

After several months I had to go to Dar es Salaam, our capital city, for some meetings. Dar es Salaam is 900 miles from Bukiroba. While I was there the Mennonite pastor, Hezekia Sarya, the man who later became the second bishop, told me that extraordinary evangelistic and healing services were being held in the Anglican Ilala cathedral. Ilala is the seat of the Tanzanian archbishop, John Sepeku.

Pastor Sarya and I went together to the cathedral. A multitude of people, 15 to 20 thousand, were gathered outside the building. Pastor Sarya told me that the meetings were supported by all the churches in Dar es Salaam. So we two Mennonites entered the cathedral and joined the scores of other clergy who were already there.

A mass healing service was something I had never seen before. I was familiar with our Mennonite service where the sick one is anointed with oil. Several months earlier I had asked some Mennonite pastors to anoint me with oil. This service had been done in my home at Bukiroba. Praying for the sick was not strange to me. But I was skeptical about praying for the sick by the thousands. Actually such a thing had never happened before in Tanzania in any denomination, so I wasn't the only clergyman witnessing something strange. I paid very close attention to what was happening. Later I checked very carefully into the story of Edmond John, the layman who was praying for the sick. Here is what I found.

Edmond John was a full brother to John Sepeku, the Anglican archbishop. Their father was a slave who had been freed by David Livingstone's University Missions to Central Africa (U.M.C.A.), an Anglo-Catholic mission. In 1967 Edmond, a deeply devout layman in his brother's church, on three successive occasions received in the night a call from God to prepare both himself and all the Christians in Tanzania to receive a guest, Jesus Christ, who was about to come into their midst.

Edmond had a good-paying job with Radio Tanzania. After receiving God's call, he resigned his job. He also sold his car because he knew that without his salary he would not have enough money to run a car. He began getting up every morning at 4:00 a.m. to pray. He followed a routine pattern—bathing, brushing his teeth, dressing in clean clothing, and then praying until dawn. He began to fast on Fridays.

Edmond lived in Dar es Salaam with his wife and family. Because of his loss of income due to resigning from his job, he moved for several months to a rural area so he could raise a crop of cardamon seed. While there, he visited a sick neighbor whose foot had been badly swollen for a long time. No one, not even the doctors, had been able to help him.

Edmond went three evenings to visit this man. On each visit Edmond prayed with him. Later Edmond heard that the man's foot had become completely well within a few days of those prayers. The man was telling his neighbors that it was

Edmond's prayers which healed him.

On hearing this, Edmond became very much afraid. Two things frightened him. One was the revelation to Edmond of God's power to heal through prayer. The second was that people might begin to think of him, Edmond, as a traditional healer, not realizing that it was the Lord Jesus himself who had healed the man's foot.

Edmond saw that the gift of healing was not an end in itself but was God's way of calling people to repentance and confession of sin so that they may come into a right relationship with God. As his preaching and healing ministry developed, Edmond was careful that it didn't get separated from the church's total ministry.

Within the circle of the church, a joint witness developed between the church's clergy and Edmond. Edmond himself asked the Lord whether he should be ordained, but God was silent. So Edmond realized that God wished his ministry to be a lay ministry, a lay ministry that was not separate from the church's clergy, a joint ministry with them. This, in brief, is the story of the man whose fluid, compelling Swahili message was calling sinners to repentance that morning at Ilala.

The cathedral was empty of people except for us clergy. Edmond John was outside on the steps at the front of the church, preaching over loudspeakers to the throng gathered there. We on the inside could easily hear what he was saying. He was calling on the people to repent and confess their sins so they might receive salvation through the sacrifice of Jesus on the cross.

Jesus was held up before the people as the Savior from sin and distress, as the Lord of all things, as Master in the lives of his followers, as the Healer of our sicknesses, as the refuge of all those who put their trust in him. The preaching was a call to the crowds to focus their attention on Jesus, God's only Son, sent to earth to live among people and to be their Redeemer. Many of the people gathered there in the streets were not Christian; thousands were followers of Islam.

After Edmond, the man of God, finished preaching, sick people were invited to come into the church. The sick came orderly by categories according to the nature of their illness. Edmond made it clear that he was not praying for people who could be healed through a medical ministry in hospitals.

He listed four categories of illnesses that were to be brought to the church for prayer: (1) Illness of the spirit such as depression caused by a person's sin. (2) Illness of the mind and emotions caused by trauma which the person may have suffered years earlier. (3) Physical illness and deformities caused by disease or by an acccident or that were congenital. (4) Illness caused by demon-possession. Edmond said that each kind of illness requires a different kind of prayer. People coming for healing had been registered earlier according to category of illness. They were now admitted inside the church by category.

For a day and night, before the beginning of the prayer services, the man of God had fasted, eating and drinking nothing. He spent the time of his fast, with others, inside the cathedral in meditation and prayer and singing. He did this so that the church might be sanctified, so that God's Holy Spirit might be free to come into every part of the building.

The people who were coming inside for prayer were not required to be Christians. But they had prepared themselves. They had been told to observe five things: (1) Confess privately to the Lord Jesus all their sin. (2) Acknowledge that it is Jesus Christ who is the Healer. (3) Be in prayer regularly morning and evening. (4) Cease forever any drunkenness and any use of tobacco. Throw away all charms and cease any association with ancestral spirits and witchcraft. (5) On the day of prayer for healing eat no food and drink no water until after the prayer for healing.

The people came into the church and knelt in rows in the large open space in front of the altar. The man of God then concentrated their attention on Jesus Christ by having them look at the cross at the front of the church. He then moved among them laying hands on each one and praying. Those who felt healing within themselves went back out the way they had come in and gave testimony over the loud-speaker of Jesus' healing. Those who were not healed went out by a side door.

Anyone was allowed to register for the prayer for healing even the Muslims, Hindus, and Traditionalists, along with Christians of all denominations. What impressed me was that so many Muslim women came into the church dressed in purdah, as they do, all in black, with their heads and faces covered. These women came when it was time for prayer for those who were demon-possessed.

Many of them began to shriek as soon as they set foot in the sanctuary. The demons became terrified of the presence of God's Holy Spirit and began to cry out. I do not mean that most Muslims are possessed of demons. No. But in the coastal East African areas, the manipulation of spiritual powers is a special characteristic of the traditional religion, and many Muslims have become involved with this. The whole sanctuary was filled with cries and shrieks as hundreds of people went out of control.

Our work as clergy was to help these people as they came in the door. We showed them the way to the front and showed them where to kneel in the open space before the altar. After the prayer, we helped those who were not able to walk to exit the church again. We worked to bring these people forward, and the man of God began to order the devils out in the name of Jesus Christ, Lord and Savior. Many were released from the demons and went out calmly by the front door to give testimony to Jesus' cleansing power.

That day I witnessed with my own eyes two healings of congenital deformities. One was a woman whose foot and hand were bent sideways. There were hundreds of people kneeling in rows in the front of the church, and the man of God was moving among them praying for each one. He would place his hands on the deformity and then he would state the attributes of Jesus Christ as Savior, Lord, King, Redeemer, Healer, having all power. Then he would pray for healing.

I watched this woman with the deformed foot and hand. I saw that on the first prayer, when the man of God prayed for her, her foot was straightened. But her hand remained deformed. When he came around the second time, he held her hand and prayed again. Then it too became straight.

The second healing I witnessed was of a small child, a toddler, who had been born blind. The child's mother brought the child into the church. The man of God laid his hands on the child's face and prayed. He then went on to others, coming again the second time and praying again stating Jesus' attributes and praying for sight for the child. Finally, he came again the third time and prayed. Suddenly the mother's face lit up with an indescribable bright joy as she cried out, "My child sees!" Immediately she went out of the church and gave witness, "Jesus has healed my child."

That series of services at Ilala lasted for one week. During that time 6,000 people were prayed for who had been preregistered. One thousand more were prayed for who had not been preregistered. A total of 7,000 people were prayed for during that week.

I was convinced that Jesus was using Edmond to speak to the Tanzanian people. I was convinced because I saw clearly that Edmond lost his own identity in Jesus when he preached and prayed for the sick. After I returned to Bukiroba, I decided to personally visit the man of God and ask him to pray for me so that I might be set free from my illness.

I traveled again the 900 miles to Dar es Salaam. On this trip I did not stay at Pastor Sarya's house. He has a large family with many children and his house was small. I stayed with another Mennonite brother, Phinehas Nyang'oro. This was sometime in 1974. I do not remember the exact date.

When I arrived in the city, I went to the house of the man of God. He conversed with me asking about my problem. He told me to eat a little that evening and then to be in prayer, confessing my sin. He told me to eat nothing and to drink nothing the next day. I was to come to him again at 5:00 p.m. the next day.

That night I did not wish to sleep. There is 24-hour electricity in Dar es Salaam, so there was light in my room the whole night. I knew what the man of God meant when he said I was to confess my sins. He meant those sins in my relationships where I am not free in my spirit with other people.

I read the Bible and prayed and sang softly all night. God put within my heart great peace. The next day I continued in prayer and fasting until the appointed time. My two brethren went with me, Pastor Hezekia Sarya, and Phinehas Nyang'oro.

When we came to the house of the man of God, he received us. He remembered the time he and I had spent together the previous day and the things we had talked about. He then told my companions that I, Bishop Kisare, had confessed my sins. He said that now the other three must confess their sins too. He, Edmond, and my two companions, were each to confess their sins in silence, each in his spirit making his confession to Jesus.

Sometimes it is not revealed to us the meaning of confessing our sin. We think that if we have not stolen or committed adultery that we have no sin. But I understood his meaning. He wished for us, leaders in the church, to be free, free in our attitudes toward each other and in our relationships in our homes and in our work. He wished us to confess to Jesus that which keeps us from peace.

The man of God then asked me where it hurt. I told him my main problem was in my chest and I was also frequently diagnosed as having amoeba. He put his hand on my chest and prayed a simple prayer, stating Jesus' attributes and absolving me of my illness in Jesus' name. I was whole and at peace. I gave thanks and praise to Jesus who healed me.

Only once after that did the problem recur. I was on an administrative trip to Mwanza. I was with Pastor Salmon Buteng'i. This was before our church center was built there. We were staying in a little hotel and I went to bathe. When the tightness came, Pastor Buteng'i asked if he should go for a doctor. I told him it was not necessary. I just sat in the doorway and soon it passed. I can still feel within me this weakness, but it has been quiescent now for all these years.

After returning from Dar es Salaam, I invited the man of God to come to Mara Region for evangelistic services and to pray for the sick. He accepted my invitation, and in February 1975 he came to us in Musoma where we held three days of meetings at the Mennonite Church in Musoma town. More than half of the Tanzanian Mennonite clergy assisted in these meetings.

At that meeting, because he was exhausted, he gave the work over to us on the third day. Over a thousand people were prayed for during the three days of meetings. Before he left, the man of God in the presence of my pastors gave me the charge to pray for the sick in my ministry.

During the time he was in Musoma, the man of God was very weak. This was the ninth series of mass meetings he had held in a period of two and one half years. A ministry of healing drains strength from the one who prays. The man of God continued to fast totally, neither eating nor drinking for the duration of his ministry at mass meetings. At Musoma he was weak even before he came and his voice was only a whisper. However, great grace was with him and many people were healed. Ours was the last public meeting he held. God took him home to heaven to be with Jesus on June 9, 1975.

The Anglican Church in Tanzania appointed a Christian brother to carefully research and document the life of Edmond John. You may read about his life and ministry in the book *Edmond John Mtu wa Mungu* by Joseph A. Namata, Central Tanganyika Press, P.O. Box 15, Dodoma, Tanzania, © 1980, pp. 147. This book is in Swahili.

Preparing ugali

LandRover

Mounds of ugali and bowls of beef sauce

Travel

So small a person I was, lost in the vastness of the Episcopal Cathedral in Washington, D.C. I sat in silent meditation. As I prayed and thought about God, I saw in my heart that this place is a human gift of adoration to the Creator. Here worship is made to God, the owner of all the wealth in the world. Here acknowledgement is made to the one from whom men and women receive the gifts of intelligence and the skills of artistry—music and color, architectural design and organization.

All the creative gifts of the Lord of the universe to mankind find expression here, brought together in one place, symbolically represented. Here man has gone to the outer limits of his ability to imagine, and out of these dreams has built an expression of adoration and praise to his Creator.

I was overwhelmed. Every facet of that building, and of the worship conducted in it, was beyond my comprehension, lifting me up out of myself to God the Supreme, the Giver of every good and perfect gift to mankind.

"*Nyasaye Nyakalaga*, I am your child, a poor and tattered peasant herdsman of Kiseru; your gifts to mankind are too wonderful for me, beyond my imagination and comprehension. Glory and honor and praise and thanksgiving belong to you forever and ever. Amen."

*I*t was my second trip outside my home country which brought me to Washington. Two years earlier, in 1959, I had journeyed to Somalia. The mission board at Salunga had sent missionaries to that country on the eastern coast of Africa to the north of Kenya. These Mennonite missionaries had come into contact with Swahili-speaking Bantu farmers along the Juba River in the southern part of Somalia.

Among the Bantu farmers the Mennonites met a number of Christian families. Long ago Swedish Lutheran missionaries had evangelized in that area. These Bantu Christians were people who had come to know Jesus Christ through the Swedish witness. The Mennonites saw that it would be good for Swahili-speaking people from Tanzania to come to Somalia to help with the evangelization of the Juba River farmers.

Elam Stauffer brought a request to our Executive Committee from the missionaries in Somalia that some of us from the Tanzania Mennonite Church visit them. We discussed this request at great length. Eventually it was decided that three pastors, Ezekiel Muganda, Nashon Nyambok, and I, should go. We three would be accompanied by Simeon and Edna Hurst and their children. We were to spend one month in Somalia, based at the Jamama Mennonite mission station.

We went overland in a pickup truck, spending a night in Nairobi and a night in Garissa on the way. I was afraid to enter Somalia because of the reputation of its people. I had heard that Somalis are fierce fighters who can kill a person and think nothing of it. We arrived at Jamama at about 4:00 p.m. and were invited into the home of Victor and Viola Dorsch. Their youngest daughter, Joy, was just one week old. They did not know Swahili so we had to communicate through Simeon and Edna, who were our interpreters.

We soon discovered that Victor was very curious about the salvation which had come to us in East Africa through the Revival Fellowship. We gave testimony in their home how God has helped us to love each other even though we come from many different ethnic groups. We showed Victor that even our team visiting Somalia had three ethnic groups— Bantu and Luo from Tanzania and Swiss German from Canada. We told him how God has even helped us in our relationships to missionaries so that we walk together with them in peace.

Victor was impressed with our testimony, but one day two of us had an argument over some little thing. Sharp words were exchanged. Victor heard the quarrel and he decided that we in East Africa are no different from anyone else. But later he saw us asking each other for forgiveness for the anger we had felt and expressed. The two who had quarreled became free and joyful again. In this way Victor understood what we had been testifying about.

Two or three days after our arrival we went to visit Brother Elisha, a Bantu Christian who knew Swahili well. We continued visiting him from time to time. He would bring the Bantu people together and we would talk with them. Sometimes a Somali would come into the meeting, only sitting there, saying nothing and leaving again. At noon we ate food in Elisha's home.

One day we crossed the Juba River to preach. Over there we met a woman named Margaret whose heart God had prepared to accept our message. That day Pastor Muganda preached. He gave the illustration of an African father who had only one daughter. This daughter ran away from home to find a good life in the city. The father went to the city. Thinking that his daughter was at the dance hall, he went there.

Standing outside near the window he whistled a song that his daughter knew. It was a song of a father's pain and loneliness and love for his child. Every night he whistled softly in the shadows, hoping that one day his daughter would be at the dance hall and hear him. For many days she was there dancing the night away, and always she heard her father's song but she would not go to him. Finally one night she could not resist his persistent love anymore, and she left the dance to be embraced by her father. Reconciled, they went home together.

Pastor Muganda said that this is an illustration of the cross of Calvary, God's persistent call to us to come back to his village. The woman, Margaret, was deeply moved by this message and she repented of her sin. The people in that place were ready to receive the gospel. Many youth and even older married people had come to the meeting.

One day we had a meeting with some Somali people. They told us that they would agree to become Mennonites, but first we must tell them what we would give them as a reward for becoming Mennonites. It was a noisy meeting. There was a lot of loud talking in the Somali language, which we could not understand.

I saw that they had not understood the message of the

gospel. This did not surprise me. I took their contention only as a noisy meeting. But afterward my companions told me that the young men were trying to pick a quarrel with us and that they were prepared to kill us. My companions had marked windows through which to escape. But I had felt no fear. I just took it to be a noisy meeting.

Before our team returned to Tanzania, we visited Mogadishu, the capital city. There we met Wilbert and Rhoda Lind. Before she was married, Rhoda had worked as a secretary at Bukiroba, so she knew us by name and we could talk with her in Swahili. We found that she had a great hunger in her soul to see African people come to salvation. Where they lived in Mogadishu no Somali believed even after many years of witness. This was because the Somali people are Muslims. We sang Swahili Christian songs for them from our songbook *Tenzi za Rohoni*, and Rhoda wept when she heard Africans singing praises to Jesus.

After we returned to Tanzania, the missionaries in Somalia asked us to send an African evangelistic couple to work along the Juba River with the Swahili-speaking people there. We knew the hunger of those people to receive the gospel. We agreed that we should send someone to them.

Somehow this vision to send a Bantu missionary to Somalia was forgotten. This made me sad—we failed to enter an open door. I think the matter was dropped because the Salunga people said we would need to support anyone who went. We weren't organized to be able to do that, so the matter was forgotten. Brother Elisha did come to visit us. He was at Bukiroba and Shirati.

My visit to the cathedral in Washington occurred in 1961 during the first fraternal visit of African Mennonites to their brothers and sisters in America. It was the leaders of the mission board at Salunga which decided that the time had come for such a visit. They wrote a letter inviting two representatives from the Tanzania Mennonite Church to come to America. Elam Stauffer called a big meeting to decide who should go.

It was very difficult to make this decision. Some thought that pastors should go. Others thought that younger, educated English-speaking schoolteachers should go. At first we thought a pastor and a teacher should go. But after several meetings it was finally agreed by everyone that Ezekiel Muganda, the senior Bantu pastor, and I, the senior Luo pastor, should go to represent our church on this visit. Neither of us could speak English, so it was decided that Simeon and Edna Hurst, who were going home for a furlough at that time anyway, should go with us.

I was surprised that the missionaries did not realize that because of our poverty we did not have respectable clothes to wear in a country like America, which is at the top of the world. When we arrived, the brethren at Salunga were embarrassed. Paul Kraybill was secretary there at that time. Bishop Amos Horst took us to the shops to get clothes for us. He told us to mention whatever clothes we wished to have. But we were embarrassed to mention our need before him. So he got for each of us two shirts, two trousers, and one coat. The coat was a plain coat, which was the style the Mennonites wore at that time. Later, students from Tanzania studying at Eastern Mennonite College boasted of their wonderful homeland, but the American students laughed at them, saying that the Tanzanian pastors needed to have clothes bought for them when they had come on a visit.

That first time that I went to the United States I was afraid to go because I considered the American Mennonites to be very holy people. It is true that some of the bishops and some of the pastors would not greet us as brothers when we attended their big meetings. But most of the bishops and pastors greeted us warmly. All the missionaries who had served in Tanzania welcomed us joyfully.

At first there was a problem to decide where we would stay while we were there. Then Daniel and Mabel Eshleman, who lived at Salunga, invited us to stay with them. The Eshlemans were very hospitable to us, showing us great love the whole time we were there. Every time I return to America, I go to visit them.

Our visit became a great opportunity for Muganda and me to give witness to the Americans of God's salvation through Jesus' sacrifice when we repent of our sin. At that time both Muganda and I were free in our relationships to each other and in the joy and power of God's saving presence.

Simeon and Edna Hurst were also joyful in the Lord and free
in their spirits toward us. So we went everywhere preaching
the good news of God's saving grace. We even preached in
Canada. To me this was the important part of our visit—the
opportunity we had to preach the gospel in many places.

People were always asking me what I saw in America
that was amazing to me, an African. Anything that is too
wonderful for me to understand fills me with joy. I delighted
in many things that I saw and experienced. One day we went
to see the horses of the Amish people. Their horses are such
beautiful animals, but the Amish do not ride them. When I
was a youth herding my father's cattle, I would ride an ox. So
I can imagine how magnificent it would be to ride a horse. If I
could, even today, I would buy a horse and ride him.

I love cattle. One day we went to see the bulls that
provide the semen for the artificial breeding program of their
farmers. One bull was so great that a lion could never kill it.
That bull would just trample a lion. When I was a boy I milked
my father's cows. The farmers in America have cows with ud-
ders as big as buckets. I wished I could have a cow like that.
Back in 1961 some people were still milking by hand, but
these days all the milking is done by machine.

Here in Kiseru country we raise tobacco, but just a few
plants. There in the Salunga area in 1961 the tobacco fields
stretched for half a mile. Their cornfields were endless and
their wheat reached the horizon. I do not know what they do
with all the food they harvest.

The cars in America are like the wildebeest on the
Serengeti Plains. There are masses and masses of cars
spread everywhere. How the Americans find the fuel to drive
all those cars is beyond my understanding. For the sake of
their cars they have extended their authority over the mountains and rivers. Anything in their path they either dig down
or they put a bridge over it. Their ability to shape the earth is
beyond my understanding.

When my wife went with me to America in 1978 for the
Mennonite World Conference in Wichita, Kansas, nothing
amazed her. I would show her the roads or buildings or fields
or animals, but nothing impressed her. She only sat sober-
faced saying that she was lonely. To her the only thing that

mattered in life was people. She was lonely for people and wanted to go home. It seemed to her that nobody lived there in America because no one conversed with her.

Then we went to Eastern Mennonite College, where we met John and Ruth Mosemann. John spoke with her in the Luo language. Ruth conversed with her. They joked with her saying that she finds America so empty a place because there are no grandchildren playing about her chair. She began to become happy again after John and Ruth spoke with her.

One day Elam and Grace Stauffer invited us to their home. Grace had prepared every kind of food that Susana likes to eat at home. After meeting with these people and eating familiar food, Susana began to laugh again. Then she was content to be in America until it was time for us to return to our home.

I have visited the United States on fraternal visits five times. Two things stand out about the second visit. That was 1967 right after my ordination as bishop. The church's executive secretary, Eliam Mauma, was with me. We attended the Mennonite World Conference in Amsterdam on our way to America.

On that trip I got an American home. Ray and Meredith Witmer invited me to make their home my home. They made me feel comfortable. Even their children were comfortable with us. We stayed there for two and onehalf months and during that entire time they never showed that they were tired of us. I did not need to be on my guard, fearful lest I do something that they would not like. I could just be myself as though I were in my own house. From that time I have called Ray and Meredith my American children. On my next three trips to America, I returned each time to the hospitality of their home.

My relationship to the Lancaster Mennonite Conference is the second thing which stands out in my memory of the 1967 visit. I had seen earlier that the mission board isn't the church. It is the servant of the church through which Lancaster Conference does its mission work at home and overseas. Now that I had been entrusted with the office of bishop, I had expected that the conference bishops would welcome me and be involved with my visit. But this didn't happen. My point of reference continued the mission board, as it had been on my first trip. Even when Mauma and I left to come back to Tanzania, it was the mission board people who took us to the airport.

So I wrote to Bishop David Thomas sharing with him my concern that I had not felt accepted by my bishop brothers in America. On my next trip in 1972, on my way to the Mennonite World Conference in Curitiba, Brazil, the Lancaster bishop brethren welcomed me and made me feel a oneness with them. When it was time for me to return home from that trip, a number of the bishops invited me tó a farewell meal where we shared together and prayed together for the work of the church.

We always flew on our trips to America. We follwed the great circle route over Iceland and Greenland, crossing from Amsterdam or London to New York. Maybe this is why I never thought about the slave ships which crossed much farther south in tropical seas sailing from West Africa to the Caribbean and Carolinas. Now on my trip to Curitiba for the Mennonite World Conference, we flew over the Caribbean to Brazil and I began to remember those ships. In Brazil I saw so many black people, and I realized that other American countries in addition to the United States have large black populations.

In the Boeing 707 whistling high above the Atlantic taking us back to New York from Curitiba, I began to weep for my brothers and sisters. There were so many of them crossing those vast reaches of water in the holds of wooden tubs, slaving ships blown by the wind in their sails. What courage of spirit, what physical fortitude, to survive the windward passage carrying with them our black seed to these lands!

In 1974 I was in the United States with Pastor Salmon Buteng'e, who was at that time treasurer of our church. That year was the celebration of 40 years since Eastern Board began work in Tanzania. I was invited to bring the spring conference sermon. I spoke on the Holy Spirit with Don Jacobs translating for me. I remember Elam Satuffer was happy with what I had to say.

In addition to their work in Tanzania and Somalia,

the mission board at Salunga had work in Ethiopia. For many years I had heard from them about the wonderful people in Ethiopia. We could tell that the mission board loved these people because from the beginning Salunga helped them to become well educated. The Americans got on well with them. At international meetings I had met some of the Mennonite leaders from Ethiopia. Once their executive secretary, Tesfatsion Delelow, visited me at Bukiroba. He was sophisticated and highly educated.

I had also heard praise for Ethiopia from my own Tanzanian countrymen. That land had received the gospel long, long ago, back near the time of the apostles. They have had their own Ethiopian Coptic Church for more than a thousand years. This country had never been colonized by the Europeans. They were always free. As Africa was struggling to become free after World War II, we looked to Ethiopia as an African country that was always free. It is true that during the second World War the Italians occupied Ethiopia, but it was only for a short time. Their king escaped to safety in England. His government continued after the war.

After many African countries became free, we organized into the Organization of African Unity and the first OAU meeting was held in the capital city, Addis Ababa. The OAU headquarters are in that city. I had heard that Addis Ababa is an old city and a big city, spread out over the mountains, with a population twice that of Nairobi, the biggest East African city.

So when the mission board at Salunga decided to have a meeting in Addis Ababa for the leaders of the Mennonite churches in Eastern Africa, I was very happy to go. I looked forward to seeing that country and to visiting my friend and brother in Christ, Tesfatsion Delelow. The Addis Ababa meeting took place in February 1976. Tesfatsion met us at the airport. He welcomed us warmly to his country and took us to the Mennonite guesthouse in the city.

One day Tesfatsion invited us to his home for a meal. I was told their food is very fiery. Tesfatsion knew that I do not like too much red pepper, so his wife reduced the seasoning a bit, but the food was still fiery. But I liked it very much and I ate a big dinner.

Their bread, *injera*, is different from our *ugali*. *Injera* is very thin and pocked on one side. It is soft and round like a flat, oversized pancake, maybe a foot and a half across. A dozen or so pieces of *injera* are spread out on a big serving platter with more *injera* rolled up, looking like rolled-up American washcloths, piled around the sides of the platter.

They put the sauce, which they call *wat*, on the *injera* that is spread in the middle of the platter. There are many kinds of *wat*, little piles of chicken, spare ribs of goat, beef, eggs, cheeses, various lentil pastes. . . . We ate by tearing off a piece of *injera*, using it to pick up bits of *wat* from the middle of the platter and putting this in our mouths. We ate and ate until we were full. Tesfatsion and his wife hosted us in a most hospitable way.

Tesfatsion has a nice home in the city. It is surrounded by a high wall with a gate at the entrance. I soon saw that all the homes in Ethiopia are built this way. Even the churches and the guesthouse are surrounded by a wall with an entrance gate.

I liked this very much. It reminded me of my boyhood home, where a fence enclosed my father's village. It is a nice way to keep your home tidy. Outside the fence is the public place that you do not worry about. Inside you may have a lawn, flower gardens, and trees with everything tidy. Inside, you are secure from the public life that goes on in the street. In Tanzania we have adopted the European way of housing with each home standing exposed to the public. This European way of housing does not appeal to me.

At our meeting in Addis Ababa we formed an association which later came to be called the Council of Eastern Africa Mennonite Churches. After the meeting, Tesfatsion took all of his guests on a trip to visit the Mennonite churches in the city of Nazareth and in the Awash Valley. In Ethiopia the Mennonites use the name Meserete Kristos Church.

The Awash Valley is part of the Eastern Africa Rift Valley. This valley extends from the Jordan River in Israel to Kenya and Tanzania. In Ethiopia the Rift Valley is an area with little rainfall, and the people living there are nomadic. A missionary doctor, Paul Yoder, and his wife, Daisy, had been working for many years with these nomadic people. On our trip we visited the area of their work. The Yoders were real missionaries of the original type: fearless in meeting new people, courageous in learning the local language and preaching to the people the gospel of Jesus Christ, compassionate in working to improve the lives of the nomads through education, medicine, and development.

In the Awash Valley I saw the oryx antelope, a herd of about twenty. They have long straight horns which are razor-sharp at the tip. Tesfatsion told us that they are very dangerous with their horns, piercing and slicing any enemy. I had great joy watching them, so proud and noble, fearless, tan with black markings.

After returning from the Awash Valley, we attended a worship service in the Nazareth church. I saw that spiritual renewal has come to these people, especially to the young people. The church was packed, but the many people crowding into the church isn't what touched my heart. It was the music of the young people which witnessed to my spirit that God was in that place.

About 30 of them sang in a choir, youth, age 15 and older. They wore robes, rust in color with white collars. Their music was lively. One of them was playing an accordion. Tears came to my eyes as I heard their singing and saw their faces radiant with joy. At that time the church in Ethiopia was in difficulty; Christians were being persecuted. But these young people were alight with the glory of God's Holy Spirit within them. I will never forget the testimony of God's presence on their faces that day. I saw that the spiritual life in the Meserete Kristos Church is within the young people.

At the time of our visit it was the dry season in the Ethiopian highlands; the harvest was in and the fields lay white, bleached by the daily sun. The Ethiopian grain is different from anything I had ever seen. It is a grass, short, of delicate fiber producing a grain so tiny that I do not see how they winnow it. Each grain is smaller than the head of a pin, less than half the size of our finger millet. In the Amharic language this Ethiopian grain is called *teff*. *Teff* flour is used to make their *injera*.

Before we left Ethiopia, Tesfatsion took us to the marketplace in Addis Ababa. It is a large area of several city blocks swarming with people. Everything is being sold in that market.

I was especially fascinated by the Ethiopian cloth. Their traditional clothing is a piece of spotless white cotton cloth woven on home looms. Each end of a length of cloth is bordered by a strip of brilliant needlework. The cost of the cloth is determined by the amount and quality of the needlework. Some pieces of cloth have borders of gold and silver thread woven into intricate patterns. The poor people use the cheapest pieces which have just an inch of bright cotton-thread embroidery at the ends—red, orange, green, blue.... I did have the money to get Susana one of the more expensive pieces.

Dressing yourself in a length of cloth is a special Ethiopian art. Susana doesn't know how to do that, so she put the piece I got for her into the box where she keeps special things.

Since that meeting in Addis Ababa the leaders of the Mennonite churches in Eastern Africa have been getting together every two years. At these meetings we share with each other what God is doing in the churches, and we encourage each other to be faithful in our lives and witness.

There are a number of Mennonite and Brethren in Christ mission boards working in Africa. Some years ago the Mennonite World Conference urged these mission boards to help the leaders of the African churches get together. This happened and an association was formed called Africa Mennonite and Brethren in Christ Fellowship (AMBCF).

When I became bishop of the Tanzania Mennonite Church, I traveled with Don Jacobs to Bulawayo, Rhodesia for a meeting of the AMBCF. That country is now free and its name is Zimbabwe, but when I went there it was still under the rule of colonial whites. I was quite frightened to go there because Tanzania was helping the freedom fighters who were struggling to bring freedom to that country. Also the white people in the whole southern part of Africa were very arrogant to us black people, pushing us around and shouting at us. There was no freedom there to talk pleasantly between white and black people. This is still the case in the

Union of South Africa.

Don and I were traveling by commercial airlines. When we came to the immigration desk at the airport, a white officer was there. He saw that I was frightened. I was surprised that he only greeted me and stamped my passport without asking any questions.

When Don and I arrived in Bulawayo, we joined other AMBCF delegates from our sister churches in Ethiopia, Ghana, Nigeria, Zaire, and Zambia. Because of that meeting, and others like it held in Nairobi, I now have friends and brothers in Christ in all these countries.

On Sunday I preached in Bulawayo. I saw that God's people were oppressed in that country by the rich and powerful white rulers. So I preached that day about Moses. He preferred to suffer with God's people rather than live a life of wealth and ease in the palace of the king. One African woman in the audience was so moved by this message that she wept openly and had to be comforted.

The Europeans had built the city of Bulawayo. They had built it up like London. There were so many things in the shops. I went window shopping, but I had no Rhodesian money, so I came home with nothing from that country.

Early morning at Busurwa

Susana Kisare, with the white head cloth, talking with a friend

Orembe, a Missionary

Susana Nyaeri, my wife, categorically refused to be operated on in that place. She begged me to take her home. If anyone was going to use a knife on her, she wanted Orembe to do it and she wanted it done at Shirati.

Susana was in the Kenyatta National Hospital, a very large referral hospital in Nairobi. We went there because the missionary doctors at Shirati advised it. They didn't want to do major surgery on my wife.

Penina, our third daughter, lives in Nairobi. Her husband, Joseph Otieno, Father of Amolo, came to the border with his car to pick us up and take us to Nairobi. You see, the border is closed between us and Kenya. It has been closed for six years now. But we can get special permission to cross on foot. So we arrange for someone to meet us on the other side.

After Susana was admitted to the Kenyatta Hospital, she saw that it was a very cold place. She had never seen the surgeon who was assigned to her case before. She insisted that she was not going to permit anyone to do surgery on her there. When I don't agree with something, I try to be rational about how I respond. But Susana just refuses, period. There is no discussing it with her.

Once you are in a hospital it isn't easy to get out again. You can't just walk out the door. People will stop you and take you back to your bed. Susana felt trapped.

When Penina's husband came to visit her, she said to him, "Father of Amolo, if you knew how tired I am, you would get me out of here. If you could get down inside of me where you could feel how I am deep inside, then you would know

141

that I am truly weary unto death in this place. You would then do what is necessary to get me out." But even Father of Amolo, important man though he is, couldn't just give the order for her release.

Actually, I agreed with Susana. Kenyatta Hospital is too big and impersonal. If people in there get well, I think it is because of their faith in God, not because of treatment. No one there knew us. Susana was just another body to them.

One of the Shirati doctors was in Nairobi at that time. He came to see Susana, to persuade her to go through with the surgery there in Nairobi. She convinced him that she wasn't changing her mind. So he telephoned Orembe.

Orembe is a surgeon at the Kilimanjaro Christian Medical Center (K.C.M.C.), Moshi, Tanzania. Realizing that Susana wouldn't be persuaded, Orembe reluctantly agreed to perform what he knew would be major abdominal surgery at Shirati on his next Flying Doctor visit.

At Kenyatta Hospital we talked to the surgeon who was assigned to Susana's case. This was mid-December. The surgeon told us that the next day he was leaving for vacation at Mombasa and would not return until after the new year. We discovered Susana's surgery had been scheduled for January 5. He told us we were lucky to have caught him before he left Nairobi. He signed the release papers so Susana could get out. Now we had to get back to Shirati.

Father of Amolo's car is rather old. It had barely made the 600-mile round trip to pick us up at the border. Some of that road is very rough, too much for an old car. I knew he could not take us back. There was no other way for us except to go by bus. Those buses are crowded and you must sit straight upright. The bus broke down on the way. It took two hours to fix it. It was a 14-hour trip to Migori, the last town before the border. The bus route ends in Migori.

We arrived at 10:00 p.m. Because the bus was late, no one was there to meet us even though the Mennonite church is quite close. So we just slept in the bus all night. Early the next morning the Mennonite pastor came and found us there. We were very cold. He arranged for a taxi to take us to his home, where his wife got us hot tea and bread for breakfast.

We had known in advance that one of the missionaries was being brought to the border from Shirati that day. So the Migori pastor arranged for us to be taken by taxi the 12 miles to the border. There we were met by the missionary LandRover, which took us the 45 miles from the official border post at Sirare to our home at Shirati. Our trip to the hospital in Nairobi took two weeks.

Orembe is a urologist. On the next Flying Doctor visit to Shirati, he was accompanied by a second surgeon, Walter Schlabach. That trip was early in January. It was 1982. On January 6 they operated on Susana.

When Orembe and Walter came into the operating room, Susana was still awake. Orembe greeted her. She told him that she was full of peace, that she had no fear or uneasiness about the operation. Then he said that she was going to be given some medicine to make her sleep. He took her hand as he offered a prayer for her, and she thought he put the sleeping medicine in her finger. But that was not true. She did not even remember the injection. The operation went well with no complications.

At the Shirati hospital patients are allowed to have a family member with them all the time. Our two oldest daughters, Margaret and Miriam, took turns being with their mother around the clock until she was fully on her way to recovery. She regained her strength very slowly. It wasn't until April that she was able to be about her normal duties. I am so grateful that we weren't in Nairobi. It would have been months and months until she would have been able to travel.

Orembe has been a special friend and brother to me for many years, and especially so since 1967 when he and his Jewish professor operated on me. That was in Philadelphia, where Orembe was on furlough studying urology. He took very good care of me. He was very gentle. I am grateful to him and his professor because they did their work well. Even up to today I have no problem from the work they did for me.

The name, Orembe, is a nickname we gave to him here at Shirati shortly after he and his wife, Lois, arrived as new missionaries in 1952. Orembe means "The Swift One." He always goes straight to the essential point of a problem, devises a plan for proceeding, and acts. No sooner does he see

a case than he is already at work solving it. Even today when
he makes a Flying Doctor visit to Shirati, the word goes right
through the hospital, "Orembe is coming. Everyone shape
up." He is terribly impatient with sloppy work, not tolerating
shortcuts to the appropriate medical procedures. We like
that about him—his insisting on professional excellence, his
professional integrity. Recently we made him a member of
our Shirati Hospital Medical Board.

Their first term of service at Shirati was five years,
1951-1957. At that time the mission board at Salunga was
very concerned about building up the church in Tanzania.
All the missionary men were ordained as pastors before they
came, even the doctors. They saw their professional work as
one facet of the total work of building up the church. Medical
work went hand in hand with evangelism and Christian nur-
ture. This is how it should be. Every missionary should know
that the church is his reason for being here.

In those days we used to do safaris with a medical van
going to isolated places, doing inoculations, prescribing
medication and preaching the gospel. We would stay a few
days at each place. These safaris were always joint efforts
contributed to equally by the church's evangelists and the
hospital's doctors. Orembe and Lois enthusiastically made
their contribution to these trips. They saw the church as important from the beginning of their time with us, and they
still see the church as important in their work.

Orembe did good work during those first five years at
Shirati. But he was very frustrated. He spent those five years
fighting Africa. We were sorry to see this because his work
was so valuable to us. But Orembe was at war those five
years. He was truly in the battle.

We Africans have a phrase, "kwa ubavu," meaning
literally "by your ribs." The English phrase "muscle your way
through" would closely express the meaning of our saying. Of
course the missionary never wins in his struggle against
Africa. So they also coined a phrase, "Africa wins again," or
just "AWA," to express this defeat. We saw Orembe in his
struggle against Africa becoming very tired and frustrated
because he did not win.

I am a herdsman. I see missionaries coming to Africa

with what a herdsman would describe as a long tether rope. Their rope is so long that they can hardly carry it. A tether rope is what a herdsman uses to tie a goat or cow so they can graze over a certain area. We do not have fences to keep our animals out of people's cultivated fields so we either put a child to watch the animals or we tether them. The resources that the missionary has are his tether rope. He comes with plenty of rope, plenty of resources.

These resources give the people from the West the ability to come here in the first place. Their resources make it possible for them to do their work and for them to enjoy Africa. If you have few resources, which is the case for most Africans, you can not do very much. You are boxed in. The people from the West not only have money so they can run projects and do things, they also have vehicles so they can travel and they have tools and radios and books.

They are well educated too, so everywhere they turn they understand what is happening, whether it be medicine, religion, development, mechanics—whatever. The missionaries always know what is happening and they get involved. So we see missionaries as people who can go anywhere and they can do anything. This is why I say that they have a long tether rope. Their resources permit them to range far and wide.

But what happens is that Africa keeps cutting off the end of the missionary's tether rope, making it shorter and shorter so that the missionary's sphere of activity becomes quite small. How does this happen?

For one thing, supplies in Africa are scarce so that, even though the missionary may have money, he can't always get the supplies he needs to do his work. Maybe the development officer can't get the right feed for his chickens—so they won't lay eggs. Maybe the doctor can't get the right medicine or doesn't have the right equipment—so the patient doesn't get well. Maybe the builder can not get cement or nails—so his project stops.

Maybe the mechanic cannot get a spare part—so his LandRover cannot travel. Maybe the teacher has a shortage of books and laboratory equipment—so he cannot fully use his teaching skills. Maybe the vacationer can't get fuel—so he must postpone or cancel his trip. Shortage of supplies prevents the missionary from using his skills and keeps him from quickly carrying out his plans. This is one way in which his tether rope is shortened.

No matter how strong or how well trained a missionary is or how many resources he can gather together, he still cannot work without getting help from other people. The missionary has to work with Africans. This is a second way in which Africa shortens his tether rope. The people who work with the missionary are not as well trained as he. They often have less experience. So, many times things go wrong in a project because of the ignorance or inexperience of the missionary's co-workers. Many things go wrong with machinery because the people using the machines are not well trained yet or they are inexperienced. The use of money as a resource in an institution is something few of us have much experience with or training for. So things go wrong and the work slows down, and the missionary often becomes angry.

But it isn't only training and experience that make it difficult for the missionary to work smoothly with his co-workers. Africa is different in many ways from the West. We do not have the same sense of time that people from an industrial country have. We do not think like a Westerner in terms of cause and effect. When we look for causes to problems, we think in terms of relationships. We look for spiritual causes. But the Westerner looks mostly for physical causes.

When a missionary becomes frustrated and angry because something was done wrong, because of a physical mistake, he often increases the emotional tension which we see as the cause in the first place for things having gone wrong. So this is a dilemma in the missonary's work, and it is one of the things which slows him down; his sphere of activity becomes smaller just because the human context here is different from what it was where the missionary came from.

Another frustrating thing for people from the West is that for us homes are public places. The more people we have around, the better we feel. But people from the West like their homes private. We keep our front door standing open. The missionary often keeps his door closed. People sitting around in his house, people coming and going frustrate him.

Those resources that a missionary brings with him combined with his need for privacy are yet another cause for his tether rope to be shortened. This is a strange reason because his resources are what give him such a big space to graze in. Yet this very thing also restricts and frustrates him. So many people go to the missionary for help for so many reasons. People go to the missionary for such things as transportation, sugar, medicine, photographs, money, clothing, tools, help in filling forms, and so on.

In some ways these requests make the missionary feel important and useful. But they also make him weary because all these things take him away from what he sees as his real work. He begins to feel that he is taken advantage of, especially when he is busy and tired. So he tries to find ways to keep people away from his door. He plans his trips without telling anyone. He may buy a fierce dog. This causes a tension between the missionary and the community. People begin to think that the missionary doesn't like them. All this makes his work go less smoothly. He finds his tether rope shortened.

But there is yet another problem, probably the greatest problem. In the West, where the missionary comes from, everyone is free to do as he likes. There are certain impersonal rules which you must follow, but otherwise everyone is free to do his work as he pleases, according to his skills and resources.

But in African society everyone has a place in relation to everyone else. For example, the only way a missionary can live in Africa is if the church has applied to the government for a work permit. The government knows that the church official who signed the work permit application is responsible for what the missionary does. So wherever a missionary works and lives, there are people responsible for him. If he doesn't know this, then his work cannot go well.

A missionary who does not know who is responsible for him and to whom he should be responsible will begin to listen to anyone's gossip, *maseng'enyo*. Consequently, he will be led by the lies and half-truths that always float about in an organization. The missionary then enters a great wilderness where anyone can push him about. His work loses its focus. His efforts become ineffective. This is because in Africa you cannot just do your work with your skill as you do in the West. In Africa, work has meaning only when it is done in the context of a community of people. If a missionary does not see clearly his community of people and their leader, then his time here and his work are meaningless, even though he may think he is doing something.

When a missionary's tether rope becomes so short, he becomes frustrated. We are unhappy to see a frustrated missionary. A frustrated missionary makes us uneasy because missionaries are such powerful people. They write letters home to their friends and to the agencies supporting our work here. They can influence how our overseas partners see us.

When missionaries are so frustrated, we cannot reason with them anymore. They see things only their own way. If there are many missionaries in one place, they can form a power bloc. None of us are present at their get-togethers, a symbol to us of their exclusivity. So they decide what to do, and they then expect us to do things their way. Then things are upside down.

Such a situation is very difficult and requires great patience, because if we react rashly, then our overseas partners will more easily listen to their missionaries than they will listen to us. So we must be very patient if there is a problem like this.

We are sorry if a missionary is frustrated because we cannot change the things that cut his tether rope so short. Our hands are tied. We cannot make Africa to be like America. We are sorry because we need the missionaries to be with us. Without interaction with peoples from the outside, we will not change. Africa needs to change. If Africa does not keep changing, then the stronger nations of the world will crush us.

We cannot be isolated. No part of the world belongs exclusively to only one ethnic group. We must learn from each other. If the missionary is frustrated, then we are no longer learning from each other. Then the purpose for our bringing the missionary to work with us is defeated.

At first Orembe fought when his tether rope became so

short; he did battle with Africa. But when he and Lois came back after their first furlough, in his sixth year as a missionary, we found him changed. His eyes had been opened. He saw his own weakness and he saw us his African brothers and sisters in Christ. He saw that we were in the same struggle he was in. Then we began to work together.

I can say this was a miracle of God's grace in his life. He was still Orembe, The Swift One. The nurses still knew they must shape up when he was around or he would shout. He continued to struggle to improve medical care at the Shirati Hospital. He still preached on Sunday whenever he had the opportunity—all these things were the same. What had changed was that now he was one with us in the struggle; he was one with us, not against us. We were no longer his problem. Now we worked together at the problem.

I do not know how this miracle happens. All I know is that in 1942, eight years after the missionaries came, God moved among us through his Holy Spirit and it was revealed to us that Jesus' blood was shed for us all so that we might all be members of one new people of God. Those of us who experienced God's blessing began to work together. And I continue to see this happening. By God's grace missionary men and women join us in the work of the church. For this ministry of theirs, I give thanks to him.

When this miracle happened to Orembe, his tether rope began to lengthen again. After three terms of service at Shirati, he returned to the United States to study urology. After certification as a urologist he served in Kinshasha, Zaire, for six years. Then God brought him back to Tanzania again.

He is now a specialist. Also Lois has a back problem and our dirt roads make that worse. So they are at K.C.M.C., Moshi, one of three large referral hospitals in Tanzania. But he still visits us at Shirati regularly via the Flying Doctor service. He is a member of our Medical Board. I am always happy to see him when he stops by my house to greet us when he is here at Shirati.

People from all over this region find their way to Shirati when they hear that he will be coming. I don't know how they find out. Somehow they know, "Orembe is coming to Shirati on such a date," and they come. I give thanks to God for my brother Orembe. Others know him as Lester Eshleman.

I am grateful to God for the many men and women missionaries who have worked faithfully with us doing Jesus' work here in the Mara Region. All my life I have worked with missionaries. By now there are hundreds of them who have worked together with us here in Tanzania. My youngest daughter, Dorika, is married to a missionary, Dale Ressler, so now I have a missionary son-in-law, *mkwerima*. I have a grandson, Martin, who is an American. They live in Harrisonburg, Virginia. I pray that God will continue to give grace to those missionaries who presently serve with us. I pray that God may call out others who will answer the call to come and be brothers and sisters with us in the work of God's kingdom.

Sunset over Lake Victoria

God Is My Portion

God's hand has been on me from childhood. I see this clearly now as I look back across the years. Earlier I did not yet see the presence of God even though he was there. The awareness came with time and on reflection.

God first spoke with me when I was still a goatherd. But I didn't know at the time that this was God's call to me. Later I saw it clearly; yes, there sitting by my mother's granary, in the early morning, when I was but a small boy, God met me. He asked me why I was here on earth. He gave me the answer to his question. I am here on earth for his purposes.

From that day onward, from time to time and in various places, I have felt God's hand upon me. Often, at the time, I was not aware of that presence, even as Jacob was not aware when he lay down to sleep in a desolate place. Jacob didn't know until he awoke that he had been in the presence of God. Even so with me; later I see it clearly that, yes, at that place, I was in the presence of God. Or there have been circumstances which later I saw were the places where the path of my life took a significant turn. Thus it becomes revealed to me that that circumstance was the finger of God.

The single most significant time that God confronted me took place 41 years ago, August 9, 1942. On that day Jesus stood before me and showed me that the path on which I walked was leading to death. I opened my life to him; he gave his life to me. That experience has been my anchor.

So many things have happened since then, so many contrary winds buffeting me about, so many great waves rolling over me, yet that anchor has held. Jesus said to me that day, "Your life is precious to me. See, I gave my life for you."

So I entrusted him with everything. Each time, when so many problems and difficulties come to me. I remember that he holds me in his hand. I give all my frustrations to him and he gives me peace. Out of that peace he gives me strength and courage for my work and freedom in my relationships.

I remember Paul. He was never afraid to admit his weakness. His triumph was not that he was strong, that he had great ability, strength, and health, no, not at all. Paul's triumph was that he rested in God's hand. The weaker he was, the more easily he saw God's hand. I use this as a model for my thinking. Sometimes my health is poor and I need to have God's people pray for me.

My weaknesses do not discourage me. I often return to Paul's testimony in 2 Corinthians 12:9-10.

> But he said to me, "My grace is sufficient for you, for my power is made perfect in weakness." Therefore I will boast all the more gladly about my weaknesses, so that Christ's power may rest on me. That is why, for Christ's sake, I delight in weaknesses, in insults, in hardships, in persecutions, in difficulties. For when I am weak, then I am strong.

I remember King David. So many enemies swarmed about David, so many difficulties to be the king. In 2 Samuel 22 David sings a song of praise to God where he speaks of God as his fortress. In five psalms he returns to this theme. One of these passages is Psalm 31.

> In you, O Lord, I have taken refuge,
> let me never be put to shame;
> deliver me in your righteousness.
> Turn your ear to me,
> come quickly to my rescue;
> be my rock of refuge,
> a strong fortress to save me.
> Since you are my rock and my fortress,
> for the sake of your name lead and guide me.
> Free me from the trap that is set for me,
> for you are my refuge.
> Into your hands I commit my spirit;
> redeem me, O Lord, the God of Truth.

Psalm 31:1-5

I praise God for the children he has given to me. These eleven children born to Susana and me, all grown to adulthood, are a great blessing. All of them are employed, some in positions of considerable responsibility. Most of them are faithful members of the Mennonite Church. All are church members.

As Susana and I grow older, our arms are shortened; we can not carry the burden of life as we once did. They rally around helping us in many ways. These days I am building my house. I do not have the resources to build alone. They have been helping me. Their money is turned to bricks in the wall of our new home. This is especially significant because, according to the traditional Luo way, when a daughter is married, she no longer contributes to her father's village. Yet our daughters have continued to remember us.

My son Abner Mosi was given the opportunity to go overseas for higher education. He got his degree and came back to help us here in Africa. Although he is now only some 30 years old, he is the Director of the Department of Rural Development for the All Africa Council of Churches. He is based at the AACC headquarters in Nairobi, but he is often on administrative trips taking him all over Africa and to Europe, Asia, and the Americas as well. Sometimes I think he lives half his life in a jet plane high above the earth.

Probably this seems to be a wonderful thing to people in the West, and it is, even to us. But, traditionally speaking, I am a very poor man because my son has not yet married. It is true that we have over 40 grandchildren, but there are no grandchildren in my village. There is no *mkamwana*, son's wife, in my village. When I think about this, the poverty of my village, I pity myself. But then God raises me up. He takes me to the story of Abraham and my soul is at peace. Abraham's portion was in the Lord who called him.

I am grateful to God for Susana, my wife, who many years ago decided to cast her lot with mine. In a few months it will be 50 years that we have lived together. All this time she has been a source of strength to me. She has always supported me in my work in the church. It is a great gift to a man when his wife joins with him forming one unit which works together for a lifetime.

Our resources have always been meager. At the beginning we had nothing at all, but at that time nothing went a long way. Now today we seem to have much but, relatively speaking, in terms of those who come to us from the outside, we are as we have always been. Susana has not resented that I was not able to give her a better life. She managed our few resources very carefully, thus making it possible for us to live and to raise our family. She was able to cook quickly a pot of *ugali* with only two sticks of firewood. I am grateful to God for gifting me with such a life companion, Nyaeri, daughter of Kimba.

I praise God for putting it into the hearts of the brothers and sisters of Lancaster Conference to carry the gospel message to a place so far from them, even to Kiseru in Tanzania. Next year it will be the Jubilee of their coming. All this time they have been faithful partners with us in spreading the gospel of Jesus Christ. I pray that God make up to them any lack or want they may have experienced through this their ministry.

When the Lord met me in 1942, I saw how good it is to be a bearer of the gospel of Jesus Christ. I praise God for the opportunities he gives me to preach this gospel in so many places. He even gave me the opportunity to carry this gospel to the United States and Canada. All of this has been God's doing. All praise and honor and glory to him forever and ever.

I do not know when I shall see him whose hand has been on my life. I pray that he keep me faithful until that day when I shall meet him face to face. Amen.

Susana Nyaeri Kisare: pictures taken ten days before her death

Epilogue

by Joseph C. Shenk

*I*n July 1981 Bishop and Mama Kisare were in Nairobi for a meeting of the General Council of Mennonite World Conference. My family had been resident in Nairobi for the previous five years. From 1963 to 1976 we had lived in Tanzania, where we worked closely with the Bishop. Our bags were now packed for our move back to the States. My last Africa assignment was to help with coordination for the General Council meeting. Bishop and Mama Kisare were among the hundred or so delegates meeting in Nairobi's Milimani Hotel.

It was the afternoon tea break. I was talking to one of the delegates when Bishop Kisare walked up and told me that Mama wanted to see me. We went over to the section of the lobby where she was sitting comfortably in an easy chair. The other chairs were occupied, so the Bishop and I stood.

"Joseph," she began, "I know that you are packed to leave Africa. But I want you to come back again. If on earth you meet someone whose blood is compatible with your blood, then it is not good for these two people to live far apart from each other. I want you to come back."

There I was standing, wondering what to say. I knew she regarded me affectionately. Her oldest daughter, Margaret, had this joke with her mother that she likes Joseph so much she can't see his faults. "Even when Joseph does wrong," Margaret used to tease, "you just say that it was an accident."

I knew, probably better than Mama, how hard it would be to get back—the difficulty of getting disengaged again

159

after beginning employment in the States, the rising costs of
international air travel, my being part of a family so that any
decision about coming back wasn't something I could do on
my own. I could have simply said, "Sure, Mama, you'll be
seeing me again before long." But she would know I wasn't
leveling with her. So I just stood there not saying anything.

"Did you hear what I said?" she finally insisted. "I want
you to come back."

At that point the Bishop said, "Of course he heard you.
He knows Swahili."

And so I said, "Yes, Mama, I have heard you."

The Bishop said, "Okay, this is why she wanted to see
you. You may go now."

And it did happen. In the rhythm of time, God made it
possible for me to return to Tanzania to be Mama's guest, on
the Shirati station, for three happy months, mid-May to mid-
August, 1983.

On July 19 she had a swollen foot. Before the doctor
could see it, she had devised her own remedy of cold soaks
and the swelling went down. That weekend, July 23 and 24,
we went by LandRover to Burere, an Ujamaa village on the
edge of the Mori Bay, for a wedding. It was one of those
weekends I could write a book about—the scenery, the
pageantry, the food, the crowds. Early the next week the doctor checked her out thoroughly and found her okay. The foot
swelling was thought to have been a phlebitis.

It was nearing the end of my visit and a number of
people began to invite the Kisares and me, with others, to
meals celebrating my visit.

On Wednesday, July 27, we were invited to a home on
the edge of the Shirati station for the evening meal. Mama
was heavy and not very active physically so we usually drove
to places. But that evening we walked. I walked with Mama,
quite slowly, coming along some distance behind the rest.
She was at her cheerful best talking with me pleasantly,
remembering past experiences.

I didn't know where the house was where we were going, and she was paying more attention to our conversation
than to the forks in the way, so we went down the wrong
path. The rest had a good laugh, shouting after us to bring

us back, breaking into our memories. After supper all of us walked back to their house together, slowly, our way lit by flashlight. It was upgrade, but not far, just some several hundred yards.

That Friday the Shirati B grandmothers' choir invited us to the evening meal. They brought the food and prepared the meal right there in the Kisare home. They did this because the Kisare home was large and centrally located for them. That afternoon Mama bathed in preparation for the evening dinner.

At the end of her bath she was suddenly seized with great difficulty in breathing and a racing pulse. The doctor came to see her, gave her medication, and told her she must rest. So we had our feast that night with apprehensive hearts. Mama was lying on the couch nearby, still with rapid pulse and breathing.

The next day, Saturday, we were invited out to both the noon and evening meals. Mama told me to eat her share. "The doctor has put me in prison," she chuckled. That same day the Bishop's half brother, Makori, came to the Kisare home to finalize plans for a dinner he was preparing. It was arranged that we go to his place on Monday afternoon.

Makori: "And you, Nyaeri, you'll be better by then and come too."

Nyaeri: "No, I am in jail now. The doctor won't let me out. But you give Joseph a leg of the ram you slaughter so I can have it prepared here and also enjoy some of your hospitality."

Makori agreed. Small talk followed. Then—

Nyaeri: "Don't forget, Makori, to give Joseph a leg for me."

Makori: "I won't forget."

Nyaeri: "And put your pick and shovel at a handy place."

Bishop: "Now, Mama, don't you talk like that."

I didn't know about this conversation until a week later.

The next day, Sunday, the 31st, there was a large church meeting in a rural area some miles away. Mama, of course, couldn't go along. As we pulled away from their home on Sunday morning, she was sitting on the front steps to the house soberly seeing us off, surrounded by her grandchildren and friends. Her special front seat in the LandRover was taken by someone else. It was a good day, but not special. Somehow with Mama not along things came across flat and pedantic.

That first week of August the Bishop had called a seminar for all the congregational leaders in his diocese. This seminar was part of the Diocesan Theological Education by Extension (T.E.E.) program in which all these leaders were enrolled. About 60 men and two women came for the seminar.

During that week Mama's spells of difficult breathing, rapid pulse, and dropping blood pressure began coming once or twice a day. The doctor diagnosed a pulmonary embolus and put her to bed with an I-V drip to thin her blood.

On Wednesday night I had a dream. A great white ship appeared on the lake sailing for shore. It seemed to be pursued. Instead of pulling up to the wharf, it drove with full power straight into the shore, plowing a great ditch and coming to rest some distance inland. Everything, both on the ship and surrounding it, was mightily shaken, things and people crashing all over the place. I was greatly frightened. Then people started standing up again, unharmed, but shaken.

When I awoke and through the next day, I was in prayer from time to time that God would spare me the pain of Mama's passing at this time, at the end of my three months with her. If the Creator was calling her home, I wished for that to happen long after I had left.

Then a quiet, calm understanding began to form in my spirit. I tried to focus my thoughts on Mama's recovery from major surgery a year and a half earlier. That recovery had made it possible for her to participate in the work of recording the story on which I had been working, to help her husband recall their life together. My prayer changed to one of thanks for God's having preserved her life long enough for us to meet again.

On Thursday afternoon all the clergy and congregational leaders who were at the T.E.E. seminar spent half an hour in prayer for Mama. That afternoon and evening she slept. But throughout the night she was in great distress.

Medical personnel from the hospital attended her around the clock right there in her home, where she was surrounded by her family and friends.

At dawn Friday morning I left by motorcycle—no fuel was available to take a LandRover—to go to Musoma, where I would inform the four Kisare daughters who lived there of their mother's illness. Before leaving I stopped by the house. The Bishop invited me into their bedroom. It was lighted by a small battery lamp. A half-dozen people were there. Mama was in great distress. She knew I was there but was unable to speak with me. My overriding impression was that it is not easy to pass through that door which opens to life in the presence of God.

Her daughters in Musoma were somehow able to get enough fuel to hire a vehicle to bring them to Shirati that same Friday afternoon. At 12:15 that night, during the first quarter hour of August 6, 1983, Mama's struggle was over.

At 2:00 a.m. someone came to waken me and Victor and Viola Dorsch, in whose home I stayed. We went together to the Kisare house.

Everything there was a shambles. The din of wailing voices made it almost impossible to hear anyone talk. Her mattress had been moved out of the bedroom onto the dining-room table. A phalanx of older Christian women, three and four deep, surrounded the table.

More people, awakened in the night, were continually arriving, adding their cry of grief to that of those already there. When the wailing would become too pandemonic or the drumming outside too overpowering, the older women surrounding the body would sing Nilotic, Christian joy songs accompanied by loud hand clapping. This added to the noise, but it did keep the chaos and confusion somewhat in check. But that first night and the next day the pandemonium was overwhelming.

Around the clock for three nights and three days those one hundred or so women took turns being with the body and working and serving the guests. There was almost continuous singing the whole time. Things were quiet only during the time the doctor treated the body with formaldehyde and Mama was placed in the white casket. She was dressed in white. A white linen cloth was on her head.

By 2:30 a.m. the night Mama died, Pastor Nashan Nyambok had called the local clergy and several church elders together for the first of many planning sessions. We met in the Bishop and Mama's bedroom, which is separated by a large room from the rest of the house. Yet the noise was so great that we had some difficulty hearing each other.

We needed to decide on the time of the funeral and on how to get the word out. The funeral time was set for Monday, August 8, at 11:00 a.m. The public telephones linking Shirati to the outside weren't working because the relay station between Shirati and Musoma was out of fuel, so the batteries had discharged. We did have radio connection to Nairobi, and the Mennonite office there could inform the daughter in the States and the two daughters in Arusha by phone, as well as Abner and Penina, who lived in Nairobi.

Arrangements were made to send someone by motorcycle to Musoma early the next morning with letters to church officials there, to the Regional Commissioner who would inform President Nyerere, and to the National Information Services so the announcement could be put on radio Tanzania. Someone else was sent to the Kenya border so the message could get to the churches in Kenya that are within walking distance of Shirati. By 3:30 a.m. the office in Nairobi had been informed. At 5:30 a.m. a LandRover left for Tarime to get timber for the casket and to take the messenger who would take the word on to Migori in Kenya. At 6:00 a.m. a motorcycle left for Musoma.

At a traditional funeral the extended family of the deceased are responsible to feed the guests who come. Already Friday night people were gathering. By the day of the funeral, their number would increase to a thousand who came from a distance and needed to be fed. Another thousand or so around the Shirati station would get food in their own homes.

A strong element in Bishop Kisare's extended family aren't Mennonites. By noon on Saturday they were insisting that the body be taken to the plot of land off the station, where the Bishop is building his house. Only then would they assume responsiblity for catering for the guests.

The Bishop didn't want his wife buried on his plot of land. He wished for Mama to be buried outside the church. It was the church, symbol on earth of God's new village, through which her life had taken its adult identity. It was within the church that she was to receive life after death and the assurance of resurrection on the last day. Her extended family in many ways had become the new people of God. So the Bishop wanted her to be buried outside the church. But burying outside the church was something which had never been done before in the Shirati area.

The local Mennonite clergy and church elders were meeting with the Bishop in his bedroom that Saturday morning. The elders of his extended family were meeting outside the house. Messages began to pass back and forth between these two groups.

As the struggle over how and where Mama was to be buried became intense, Victor Dorsch and I asked to be excused from the group that was meeting in the bedroom. We felt that the traditionalists would say that the Western missionaries were influencing the crucial decisions. The other brethren there agreed with us, saying that in order to protect the integrity of the decision-making process, they would accept our offer to withdraw.

They called us back after three hours. During the time we were out, it had been decided that Mama would be buried next to the church. This meant that the church was agreeing to carry the full weight of catering for the guests. From the moment the Bishop saw that the church was rallying behind him, he began to regain his strength and resolve. He was no longer totally devastated by the death he was experiencing.

The drumming continued off and on right up to the time for the Sunday morning worship service, and men with spears and shields, warriors dressed in battle regalia, were circling the house. Someone took a young black bull into the room where Mama lay. But the intensity of that element slowly faded. Before the funeral on Monday, many of the Bishop's relatives came over to his side, supporting him in his decision.

As more and more clergy and church leaders arrived from a number of denominations, they continued to strengthen the Bishop by encouraging him to keep the proceedings Christian. "If you buckle," they said, "then we will be swept away. But if you hold firm, you will strengthen us for the day when we will face the same issues."

Right from Saturday morning people from the Shirati station and environs began bringing food to the Kisare home. Some of it was in the form of tea and doughnuts. Some of it was cooked meat—beef, chicken, fish. Some of it was flour for making gruel and *ugali.* Women quickly set up a cooking area out back of the house.

A fund was established targeted at about $800 to buy a bull, sugar, flour, salt, and other food, for the main meals on Sunday evening, Monday morning, and Monday afternoon. During that week of the funeral and the following month, 17 animals were donated as the church and many people from the Bishop's extended family rallied to his need. Only one bull from the Bishop's personal corral was butchered.

Each aspect of the activity in and around the Bishop's house had a specific person assigned to it. Pastor Nyambok as chairman of the planning committee had overall responsibility. The hospital administrator, Jeremiah Okidi, was the coordinator of activities. There was no lack of money or food or willing hands to do that mountain of work.

Each of the two nights of the wake a worship service (choirs, testimonies, scriptural meditation, announcements concerning procedures and catering) was held in the open area in front of the Bishop's house. The benches from the church were brought over to the house for the night service the evening before the funeral. All the benches were full with many more people inside the house and many others standing outside, just hundreds and hundreds of people. The Bishop's relatives by the hundreds were on one side of the house; Mama's relatives covered the area on the other side; the rest of us filled the area in front of the house.

That night the service didn't start until nearly 10:00 p.m. About an hour before the service everything became quiet—no wailing, no drumming, no counter-action Nilotic joy songs, just a great silence. It was a cool evening, perfectly still air, cloudless star-studded sky—the Milky Way climbing like a broad ribbon of white across the sky horizon to horizon, north to south, rising with the turn of the earth out of the east, spread overhead by the time we disbanded at midnight.

I was standing back in the shadows away from the light of the pressure lantern hanging beside the doorway to the house. Flashes of Mama kept coming back. A number of times we went to the Serengeti National Park together. Once we went with the Shirati B choir and that time I headed off a herd of running cape buffalo with the LandRover, frightening Mama so much she ordered that I stop.

Once during the year I was their driver, they had a trip to Nairobi, and Mama invited my wife, Edith, to be her guest and go along. On that trip her daughter, Penina, who lives in Nairobi, had given her a new blanket. Mama was worried that the customs people at the Tanzania border, on our way home, would give her a rough time about the blanket. They didn't say a thing, but they did ask us to take someone with us to the next town. As soon as we cleared the border post, Mama engaged me in conversation, keeping it up until our passenger had been discharged. She then asked with a grin, "Do you know why I kept talking to you?"

"No," I answered.

"That man who got in the car was a plain clothes detective, and I didn't want you to go talking about my blanket."

This is how Mama was. She was insightful, and she would gently take charge of a situation without your being quite aware of it. She knew all about everything that was going on. Yet for all that she knew, I never heard her say anything unpleasant about anyone.

Mama used to joke about holding court. That was when the children would bring their cases against each other for her adjudication. She would sit in her chair on the tiny veranda at the back of the house and listen to their arguments and then dispense a bit of firm grandmotherly common sense.

Mama had her office. It was back in the kitchen part of the house. There she would sit in her wicker chair and supervise the culinary activities. Just a week before her death she was there supervising the preparation of dried beef for me to take back to the States for her daughter in Virginia. She even gave me a lesson once on the preparation of Nile perch.

In her office all was well if her emergency barrel was full of water (in case the station supply got cut off), if she had a sack of ground grain, and if her woodbox was full. As long as she had those three essential raw materials, she could handle anything.

Twelve-year-old granddaughter, Edith, whose father was killed in a car crash some years ago, prepared the last meal I had with the Kisares. It was all done under Mama's watchful eye, of course. Mama wouldn't tell "Baba," as the Bishop was called at home, until after we had eaten and praised the texture of the *ugali* and the seasoning of the beef. Then she told us with a chuckle, daring us to say it had been prepared by an amateur.

Mama's office was her schoolroom where for almost half a century she'd been teaching girls how to cook. Early in her married life she was almost embarrassed when people began calling her "the teacher's wife," not realizing how good a teacher she was herself.

I used to think that I had a special relationship with her, but as time went on I found out everyone felt this way about her. She looked out for everyone and somehow made us all feel special. She saw herself as mother to all peoples— Luo, Bantu, Canadian, American—she treated everyone with respect and common sense. She tried, with humor, to greet everyone in his mother tongue. She saw people's strengths and refused to participate in gossip.

On occasion Mama would argue with her husband. I remember once a new missionary wanted to be given three months off from his work to go to Swahili language school. The ensuing conversation went something like this:

Mama: "That wouldn't be very useful. You can't learn Swahili in a school. What you should do is visit your neighbors in the evenings and talk with them. Then you will learn Swahili."

Bishop: "Mama, you don't understand these educated people. They can learn a language in school. They learn a language through books."

Mama: "That is foolish to learn a language with a book.

You read a book with your eyes. The eyes do not hear how people talk. Language is done with the ears, not the eyes."

Bishop: "No, Mama, these educated people can hear through their eyes."

Mama: "Don't be foolish."

The Bishop won that argument. The missionary went to Swahili school and became one of the best Swahili conversationalists I know, so good in fact that he could persuade Mama to let him marry her youngest daughter, Dorika.

The funeral was Monday morning. Somehow people found diesel fuel to get their LandRovers on the road. Supplies put aside for emergencies came out of back rooms. People continued arriving up to after the 11:00 a.m. service had begun.

They came from the Nairobi and Migori church districts in Kenya. They came from the Bumangi, Mugango, Mugumu, Bukiroba, and Musoma church districts in South Mara. They came from all over the Bishop's own North Mara Diocese. Bishop and Mrs. Hezekia Sarya of the South Mara Diocese came. The regional commissioner came as personal representative of President Nyerere. An old friend of mine remarked, "This Mama called a lot of people together, didn't she?"

At a time like that, one becomes the property of the public. The church service and the viewing which followed the service lasted four hours. Bishop Kisare sat there in his chair the whole time, getting up only once to tell us what a wonderful wife Susana had been to him and to thank everyone for gathering around to strengthen his faith.

The church was packed, aisles and window ledges full. Outside there were more people than inside, some 2,000 people in all. A loudspeaking system allowed those on the outside to participate. There were so many people to make speeches, so many remembering with joy Susana's life, so many choirs to sing.

Pastor Manaen Wadugu prayed, "Father, we do not look back, we do not ask why. Rather, we look forward. We look to you, the Savior, who picks us up when we fall. We ask you to hold our Bishop's hand. We trust you to take him safely through this great tribulation which has come upon him. We ask you to receive our sister and mother who has left us. Keep her in peace until the resurrection day. Amen."

Susana's older sister is blind. A month before when we were at Ligero, I had taken Mama to visit her sister who lives in that area. Mama gave her sister a new *kitenge* cloth. She called Mama "Akello," remembering that Susana was born after twins. The sister said, "The blind and lame last a long time. I'll still be here for a while. So you come visit me again."

At the viewing following the speeches I saw this old woman, this blind sister of Susana's, with her stick, in the line that was coming in from outside the church. She had just arrived; she had walked 21 miles to get there. She couldn't see but she knew the contours of "Akello's" face. She paused to "see" her sister, but only for a moment. She had to hurry along, so many others were pushing from behind, wanting to see too.

Later, after all the tumult was over with the grave filled in and everyone gathered for the meal back at the house, I saw her, Susana's older sister, sitting alone on a stone on top of the grave, crying softly to herself.

Three of the Bishop's daughters arrived after the funeral. Lois and Ruth came by Missionary Aviation Fellowship light aircraft from Arusha, arriving at about 5:00 p.m. Dorika with her husband and son arrived later that night, bringing with them messages of condolence from the Mennonite Church General Assembly meeting in Bethlehem, Pennsylvania, from the Lancaster Conference bishops, and from the Eastern Mennonite Board of Missions. They had flown by commercial airlines from Washington, D.C., to Nairobi via London. From Nairobi they came by car to the border where they were allowed to pass because of the exceptional circumstances. All of the Kisare children, except Tereza who lives in Kigoma and couldn't get transportation right away, were together with their father the evening of the day of the funeral.

Traditionally, in the Luo society, at the death of a woman, close relatives and friends remain in the village of the deceased, comforting the bereaved, for a period of four days following the funeral. I had to leave Shirati on Saturday to catch my flight from Musoma at the beginning of my trip back to my family in the States. The timing of Mama's funeral allowed me the four days of mourning plus one.

During those several days before I left, two grandmothers from the Shirati B choir sought me out. They came to my room. We all sat down.

"Joseph," they said, "do not return to your family with a heavy heart. We knew Mama well, better than you ever could. We know how she would have you view her homegoing at the time when you were her guest. She would have you accept this as a blessing to you, a blessing because you were with her on her last journey."

(Above) Shirati B Grandmothers' Choir. (Right) Director of a youth choir. (Below) Youth, with a drum, singing.

Appendix

Safari with Bishop Kisare

by Joseph C. Shenk

If I were a youth coming to faith in Jesus Christ today in Kiseru, what would I be experiencing? What is the message in sermon, song, and community? Here is the text of four of Bishop Kisare's sermons and an account of present-day hymnody set in the context of three weekend, church-sponsored youth rallies.

Ligero, Buturi

Eight-thirty in the evening. It had been dark for an hour and a half already, and we still had not eaten. To the north lightning was flashing and a steady wind was coming off the higher elevation east of us, blowing toward the lake 14 miles away. We sat huddled in sweaters and blankets, some of us just huddling, body to body, against the chill imminence of a good soaking.

A swaying kerosene pressure lantern lighted up the place where we sat, outdoors, under a canopy of reed mats and dried tree branches. This *banda* or shelter covered a large grassless area between two mudbrick thatched houses; our shade from the sun during the morning and afternoon evangelistic services now offered only a psychological sense of being inside.

Tables, a score or more, had been brought from the surrounding homes, tables of all sizes and types for serving food on. Chairs were drawn up here and there forming circles around the tables. The *banda* was full of people waiting for supper. We sitting there were Bishop and Mama Kisare, with their evangelistic team, and five choirs from as far as 20 miles distant.

173

The rain could hold itself off no longer, sprinkling first, chasing us to cover in nearby houses, and then bucketing down, dousing all the cooking fires under our three-quarters prepared supper and turning everything into a sea of mud.

Well, that was that, as far as having an evening youth rally was concerned. It poured for half an hour and then drizzled for another 30 minutes before the cooking brigade could get organized again for another go at getting supper ready. Finally at 10:30 p.m. food was served. We were back in the *banda,* mud now on shoes and bare feet.

By 11:15 p.m. we guests, some 150 of us, had eaten supper and washed our hands clean from the meal. Someone prayed the prayer for close of day, and we all went off to our designated places of sleep, leaving the mess of bowls and plates for our hosts to clean up.

This was the second night of a three-day evangelistic safari to Ligero. It had rained heavily the first night too, only it rained earlier that time, most of it before dark, so our night rally had not been aborted. It was most extraordinary to have any rain at all in the beginning of July, let alone cloudbursts and on successive evenings.

In the mid-70s all peasants in Tanzania were moved by the government from their scattered dwellings to collectivized villages called familyhood villages, or *ujamaa* villages. Each family has up to two acres on which to build houses and cattle corral, to plant trees and till a vegetable garden. Some 200 families comprise one *ujamaa* village.

Areas around the housing concentration are designated for cattle grazing and agriculture with land allocation being made by the village council. An outstanding side effect of having people living in a concentrated area this way is that primary education is now accessible to everyone, and Tanzania has the highest literacy rate in Africa, 80 percent.

Ligero is the easternmost *ujamaa* village in the Buturi chain of such villages. A month earlier on an overland hike from Shirati to Bukiroba and back, I had spent the nights, going and coming, three miles west of Ligero toward the lake.

That Buturi plain, to my mind, is pretty dull and uninteresting, a cattle area with few trees, grass eaten off, boxlike houses sitting here and there, an occasional one of cement block with a metal roof, most of them mud-walled with grass roofs. The people are not so poor; it is just that the goats, sheep, and cows eat everything off around the houses, and there are no rock piles to break up the monotony of the landscape.

Why were we there, a handful of preachers and a half-dozen choirs, spending a weekend of singing, preaching, and eating on the

Buturi plain? Some weeks earlier the Ligero choir had been invited by the Nyabikondo choir to spend a weekend at Nyabikondo. Nyabikondo is about halfway between Ligero and Shirati, a ten-mile distance for the Ligero youth to hike over to Nyabikondo. Well, one invitation requires a return invitation, so a weekend was set for the Nyabikondo choir to visit Ligero. That is how our weekend got started.

The evangelist at Ligero, Emmanuel Oudu, saw the choir visit as an opportunity to have a community evangelistic effort. Oudu got his congregation together, and they decided to make a really special weekend of it by inviting Bishop Kisare and his wife, Susana, to come. The Ligero choir had already purchased a ram to feed their guests. Emmanuel pitched in with a young bull from his herd. The elders of the congregation passed the hat and got a second ram. So with that much meat they began to think really big.

In addition to the Nyabikondo choir they invited the Gor Maia choir from the Shirati church and the Mikondo choir. The Mikondo choir has two guitars and an accordion and is generally considered the best choir in the North Mara Diocese. That is the oldest choir. Mikondo began singing 20 years ago.

Both Gor Maia and Mikondo had 21 miles to walk one way to get to Ligero. Oudu and his congregation also invited the pastor of their church district, Gershon Ayoo, and the choir from Ayoo's church at Utegi, the Kibachiro choir. This choir from Utegi walked 14 miles one way.

To top off the guest list Bishop Kisare was asked to bring with him the Shirati B choir. Shirati B is composed of seven grand-mothers who are extraordinarily gifted in putting the Christian message to the ancient Nilotic minor-key rhythms of dirge or festival. They are barely literate. They do the composing and carry the music in their heads. They are seven saints who are sheer joy to be with. Bishop Kisare also invited three pastors to accompany him—a Luo grandfather, Dishon Ngoya; a young Luo schoolteacher, Lawrence Saidi; and me, his guest.

I figured up that the youth in the choirs walked a total of 2,508 miles going to Ligero and back that weekend. Of course Shirati B and we three pastors got seats in the Bishop's LandRover along with Mama Susana. Up on the roof rack we had two tents, cots, and bedding, and the overnight bags for ourselves and the 27 members of Gor Maia, who had set out from Shirati before daylight.

Many of the families on the Shirati station have children in Gor Maia. Bishop Kisare himself has three grandchildren in the choir. The choir mentors are young married employees of the hospital.

Our splay-legged LandRover pulling out of Shirati that Friday morning bore a festive crowd. Shirati B struck up a joyful travel song lined by Lawrence's strong baritone from the back seat.

A Traveling Joy Song
(Sung with syncopated hand clapping)

Leader: Eeee Jesus Savior,
Chorus: Eeee you having life,
         Others are announcing Jesus Savior, we too announce him.

Leader: To Kirogo we went in the Holy Spirit,
Chorus: Eeee you having life,
         Others are in the Holy Spirit, we too are in him.

Leader: Eeee to Burere we went bearing the gospel,
Chorus: Eeee you having life,
         Others are bearing the gospel, we too are bearing the gospel.

Leader: Eeee I'm praising my Jesus,
Chorus: Eeee you having life,
         Others are praising Jesus, I too am praising him.

Leader: Eeee I'm confessing my sins to Jesus,
Chorus: Eeee you having life,
         Others are confessing to you, I too confess to you.

Leader: Eeee at Ligero we'll sing of salvation,
Chorus: Eeee you having life,
         Others are singing of salvation, we too will sing.
Et cetera ad infinitum.

These people sing in the open air without mikes so they've got power and can turn the decibels right up. The festive songs are accompanied by hand clapping, four fingers against hollow palm cracking like rifle shots. They do this with syncopation, two levels of rhythm. All that is great, out in the open air; in the confines of a LandRover, well, I was glad to have the windows open.

The LandRover and choirs all arrived at Ligero toward evening at about the same time. There were great eight-foot lengths of sugarcane for the youth to cut up and chew, sweek milk-tea and yams for everyone. With the rain and all we didn't get supper over with until 9:30 that night. Things were pretty dried off by then, and we went ahead and had the planned youth rally. Each choir sang one song, that's all. It took us till 11:30. In addition to the guest choirs, Ligero fielded two home choirs, and the neighboring Mennonite church, Nyakoba, fielded one.

Each choir number is a whole drama, not just a song. When it's their turn, a choir lines up outside the *banda* in two rows. Each choir has three rhythm instruments—a metal ring six to eight inches in diameter struck with a large nail or bolt, a small hand-held drum or two, and a rattle.

The metal ring can be made to vary its contribution by how it is held—full-fisted for a dull ring, one-fingered for more brightness, and a tossing movement giving a clear note suddenly dampened. The drum provides a fundamental beat, dull, steady, done with the ball of the hand accompanied by an overlay of pings and pops put in with the fingers.

The rattle is a rectangular box an inch deep by twelve inches long and six inches wide. The top and bottom are made of slats of thick grass stems. Inside are little crimson seeds with black eyes, about the size of popcorn kernels. The rattle is shaken between the two hands in such a way that the seeds slide swooshing against the ends of the rattle or stop midway in the box, thus producing its own syncopated beat. The Bishop leaned over once and whispered in my ear, "Could you stop those seeds midslide like that? I've tried and I surely can't."

When the choir is ready, the steel ring sets the beat joined next by the drum and then by the rattle. Once those syncopations are harmonized, singing begins. After the rhythm of song is established, on a signal from the director, often the smallest member of the choir, everyone together begins a footbeat—right, left, accompanied by a swaying body bounce and arm movement.

In the traditional dance the footbeat is a sliding movement forward creating a swoosh sound followed by a flat clap of foot to ground. It is two steps forward, one backward, creating a drumbeat of foot on earth. But in the church dance, the foot swoosh-ka-beat is almost inaudible, just faintly there. The back step is eliminated.

Once everything is in harmony, the choir moves into the arena, wheeling the two columns into place in the middle of the *banda*, usually facing the side where the elders are seated. When all members are in place, the music stops. Then it begins again on a new rhythm, the one of the song to be sung—first the steel ring, then the drum and rattle, followed by song and footbeat.

When the song is finished there is silence once more. Then the exit dance is programmed—steel ring, drum, rattle, song, footbeat, wheeling into columns, slowly out of the arena, giving way to the next choir which is already lined up waiting to begin. Thus each choir gets three songs—one on entry, one for the actual performance, and one on exit.

Night youth rallies are *ujamaa* village happenings. People come from several miles away. Easily a thousand gather at this, the social event of the month. Occasionally a few drunks show up shouting noisily, but usually everyone is quiet and orderly, listening to the gospel message in song. When the evening is over, people quickly disperse, with the visiting choirs going to previously assigned places to sleep, girls to one house, boys to another, reed mats on the floor; they roll up in sheets and blankets for sleep.

Pastor Ayoo was master of ceremonies. He had a whistle that he blew every time he had something to announce. At 5:30 Saturday morning, an hour before daybreak, he blew his whistle, standing outside the house where he had slept. Then in a high, loud voice he announced the new day, calling our hosts to get up and begin their various ministries.

Many tasks awaited them. Water had to be carried from the nearby dam. Last night's scores of bowls and drinking vessels must be washed before serving breakfast. Fires were to be lit in the out-side cooking area to boil water for tea and gruel. Tables and chairs needed to be rearranged from last night's meeting; every sleeping place needed to be provided with a bucket or pitcher of water for washing hands and faces and brushing teeth. A ram and bull waited to be butchered. There was much work to be done.

It was great being a guest and just listening to Pastor Ayoo as he walked some 200 yards from where he had slept, calling out the program for the day and generally alerting the *ujamaa* village sleep-ing around us that something interesting was afoot. Before he was through I had rolled over in my warm sleeping bag and had gone back to sleep again, awaking an hour and a half later when a teaket-tle of warm water showed up outside our tent flap so we three pas-tors could wash our faces and brush our teeth.

The new day was clear, windy, cold. Mama Susana hadn't figured on rain and this sharp east wind. She hadn't even brought a sweater. After the rain the night before, she stayed in their tent wrapped up in her bedroll, eating supper from a tiny table the servers brought for her. Now at the call for breakfast she was back in the *banda*, whipped by the wind and shivering cold. We found a bright blue nylon sleeping bag which we wrapped around her shoulders, our plump little queen warm and happy again, ready for our breakfast of tea and bananas.

The morning singing and preaching service got underway by 11:00 a.m. Half the choirs had one song each before the sermon. The second half sang at the end of the service. Bishop Kisare opened his message with a prayer asking God to direct his thoughts so that his message might fit the situation at Ligero.

In brief, this is what he said: "The gospel has been preached in this land for a very long time. I, a child of Kiseru, assure you of this. Even before the Mennonites came, the Adventists were preaching here. But when I look at the people here at Buturi and at Shirati, I find that this preaching of the gospel has made no difference at all. People still live as they always did following in the traditions of their ancestors. Why is this? There has been no change because people have not realized what the gospel is about. Let me tell you this morning what the message of the gospel is.

"In Luke 9:30, 31 we read that Jesus was on a mountain, and while he was there Moses and Elijah came to talk with him. Moses and Elijah had been buried long before this. They were among the long-departed Hebrew ancestors. Why now have they reappeared? In their lives they saw into the future that God would bring salvation to people. They set the stage for the coming of this salvation. They saw into the future that God would bring salvation through the sacrificial death of his Son Jesus.

"The death of Jesus is the central subject of the Bible. It is mentioned 175 times in the Bible. Moses and Elijah saw that the moment is about to come when sinners will be freed, when all of nature will be freed, freed from the curse which sin brought into the world. They were so happy to see the time for redemption draw near that they came back from the dead to talk with Jesus. They wanted to encourage him to finish properly the work which had brought him into the world, the work which would bring to completion the worship systems of the ancestors.

"You remember the story in the Old Testament when Elijah had the contest with the prophets of Baal? From the time of Moses, when people sinned, they would take a sheep or ox and burn it to ashes to show to God their repentance. Even with us in our Luo traditional worship we did this.

"No fire came to burn the animal that the priests of Baal had put on their altar. Those priests were only praying to the ancestors who could not help them at all. But when Elijah prayed, fire came from heaven and burned up everything, even the bones and the stones. Elijah's sacrifice that day was accepted by God because it was a prophecy of the coming sacrifice which Jesus will make. This is why Moses and Elijah came to see Jesus, because their prophecies were now close to fulfillment. The day for people to be freed was at hand.

"People take Jesus' death as a traditional religion. They do not realize that in his death is the power to set them free. So this is why nothing has changed in all these years since the gospel has been preached in this land. People think that those who preach the gospel are just doing it to benefit their own villages. I Peter 1:12 makes it clear that those who preach the gospel do it for the benefit of those on the outside who hear and not for their personal benefit.

"I do not preach the gospel the way a farmer sells sugar cane.

The farmer sells his sugar cane so he can get money to benefit himself and his village. Preaching the gospel is not this way. We preach in the hope that you, people for whom I would have no concern in the traditional way, will understand and accept the message and be set free to become part of God's new family. Even if only one person receives this message and is set free, then this land of Buturi is blessed.

"God's people who have already died, millions and millions of them in heaven, are continually singing the praises of Jesus whose sacrifice set them free. At the moment of Jesus' death, at the ninth hour, there was a quaking of the earth, the soil itself and the trees cried out in joy. Why? Because from the time of Adam's sin, all of creation was under a curse. Now Jesus has set creation free and the earth, trembling, cried out, 'Son of God, you have returned us to our former state!'

"All of the religious things we do only box us in if we have not understood and appropriated Jesus' sacrifice for us. This I know is the truth, that through Jesus, those fences which held us in our traditional circles were torn down and we were set free to enter into a new and right relationship with each other and with God.

"This work of Jesus is a miracle. How can I explain it? Take a cow. I do not know how a cow can eat grass and drink water and produce milk. It is not for me to know how that happens. All that is needful for me to have health is to milk the cow and drink the milk. The lake is full of water. I do not know how the water came to be there or of what water is made. To have life I do not need to know these things. All I need is to go to the lake with my vessel, draw and drink. This is how it is with Jesus' sacrifice. It is the power of God to save us. How it happens I do not know. What I know is that when I appropriate that sacrifice I am made whole.

"Paul makes an effort to describe this in Romans 11:33-34:

'Oh, the depth of the riches of the wisdom and knowledge of God!
    How unsearchable his judgments,
        and his paths beyond tracing out!
Who had known the mind of the Lord?
Or who has been his counselor?'   Amen."

The first night of the conference the kerosene had run low. So at dawn's first light a young chap had been sent off to Kenya by bicycle to get a gallon of the precious liquid. He followed a cross-country route using cattle trails and footpaths crossing into Kenya somewhere between the lake and the official border checkpoint at Sirare. Our young 15-year-old courier must have ridden 70 miles that day, bringing us a gallon of fuel so our pressure lantern could light our activities the second night of the conference.

Sunday morning 387 people attended the worship service. Choirs sang. Just before the Bishop brought the morning message, he asked the grandmothers of Shirati B to sing his favorite dirge.

A Passion Dirge
(Sung without clapping in a minor Nilotic key)

Eeee Jesus whom we love, Come enter my place.
We call on you Hosanna the holy one, Come enter my place.
The Lion of Judah goes forth
    In his holiness;
    We sing to him hosannas, Come enter my place.

Long ago they waved palm branches for you,
    Carpeting all the paths
    Carpeting also with sleeping mats,
Singing to him hosannas with ululation.

    Eeee Hosanna is going in his glory,
    Hallelujah to Hosanna the holy one,
    You deserving adoration,
    We open our hearts to you, Come enter my place.

Awaking from last night's sleep to face the people's dreadful judgment,
    The donkey never climbed upon,
    He called then for that donkey,
If the people ask you, say the Lord wants him to ride upon;
The day he rode upon the donkey
    He announced his kingship
    A revelation he hadn't made before.

    Eeee Hosanna is going in his glory,
    Hallelujah to Hosanna the holy one,
    You deserving adoration,
    We open our hearts to you, Come enter my place.

Jesus bore the timber staggering beneath its weight,
    The Lion of Judah goes forth
    To finish the battle,
That day the angels were amazed asking what sacrifice this,
What mandate requires the Son of God
    To go to his slaughter,
    Defenseless in the hands of savages?

    Eeee Hosanna is going in his glory,
    Hallelujah to Hosanna the holy one,
    You deserving adoration
    We open our hearts to you, Come enter my place.

Having within him the strength of Judah
    He shatters the tomb in the morning,

> He shows himself 40 days to the world,
> That day Thomas accepted
> All the disciples were filled with joy
>   For *his* judgments
> Have conquered the whole earth.
>
>   Eeee Hosanna is going in his glory,
>   Hallelujah to Hosanna the holy one,
>   You deserving adoration,
>   We open our hearts to you, Come enter my place.

"The words you sing, you young people in your choirs, are of great wisdom and grace. For in song you proclaim that God is calling us to enter a good place, the Land of Promise where milk and honey flow, where two harvests a year are normal, where the hills are full of silver and everyone has plenty to eat. For anyone who has entered this land, it is his responsibility to tell others about how to get there too.

"This is our sin against the people of Buturi. We have found the place of plenty and blessing, yet we have not returned to tell others. We enter the Promised Land, but no witness goes back to those we left behind telling them how to enter too. These people here at Buturi, I cannot fault them for living in darkness. If they would kill me for hiding from them the secret of life, I could not blame them. Salvation has not covered this land because we who have received grace have not gone back to tell others.

"Consider the enormity of God's act to set us free. What salvation is this that Barabbas, a murderer, is set free so that savages may slaughter God's holy Son? Jesus' blood which was poured out for us, this unfathomable statement of God's reconciling love, is the cement which can hold the nations together in one new nation of God.

"Consider Colossians 2:13-14. 'When you were dead in your sins ... God made you alive with Christ. He forgave all our sins, having canceled the written code, with its regulations, that was against us and that stood opposed to us; he took it away, nailing it to the cross.' This is how I, Kisare, have been set free from all condemnation, personally set free, but at so great a price. To set me free could not be done for a pittance; it required the blood sacrifice of the one good man who ever lived.

"On the cross Jesus cried out, *'Eloi, Eloi, lama sabachthani?'* which means, 'My God, my God, why have you forsaken me?' This was as the cry of a mother giving birth. At the moment of birth she hangs on the brink of death, all else smothered from her awareness by the enormity of her individual lonely pain; she cries out in desolation as the child is brought forth. This was the passage through which Jesus went in birthing salvation.

"Consider Ephesians 2:14-16: 'For he himself is our peace, who has made the two one and has destroyed the barrier, the dividing wall of hostility, by abolishing in his flesh the law with its commandments and regulations. His purpose was to create in himself one new man out of the two, thus making peace, and in his own body to reconcile both of them to God through the cross, by which he put to death their hostility.'

"The world is full of ethnicity, each group of people defining its boundaries with its own traditional codes of pride, prejudice and arrogance. Wherever you see quarreling and hostility, there the blood of Jesus has not been appropriated. Jesus' blood is a great bulldozer smashing down the walls of hostility which divide people on this earth, a bulldozer of enormous value created through God's own unspeakable suffering at the hands of heartless savages.

"How has this happened? I do not know. How does a cow give milk? I do not know. To live I do not need to know how a cow produces milk; all I need to do is milk the cow and drink. I do not need to understand God's redemptive act for me, all I need to do is accept it, allowing his redemptive power to continually transform my life. Amen."

An invitation was given with scores of people responding.

Before the service a woman had asked the Bishop to pray for her and her child. This woman has had many children but they all died in infancy. Now again she has a daughter who is six months old. Before the close of the service she came forward, and the Bishop prayed for her, asking our Father/Creator to preserve this child to the age when she will go to school, to the time when in the mother's own old age this child will care for her.

By the time we had had lunch it was 3:00 p.m., far too late for the choirs to begin their nine-hour hike home. The Ligero youth invited the choirs to stay over for the night beginning their return journey after breakfast the next morning. After all, a third of the bull had not yet been eaten, and there was still kerosene for the pressure lantern. So they stayed while grandmothers, pastors, and bishop couple packed into the LandRover and set off home, waved off by a great throng of God's people.

As I backed around with the LandRover, I almost ran over a battered, blue, tractor gas tank, the only remains of an old Mennonite Economic Development Associates (MEDA) project. That would make another good story, if it were told.

Kirongwe

A weekend earlier Bishop Kisare had taken me with him to Kirongwe, the place on the lake two miles from the Kenya border where he spent his happy boyhood. He took me to see his father's grave. Kirongwe is only 10 miles from the Shirati station and a good road runs up there stopping just short of the Kenya border at the Kirongwe Primary School.

The conference that weekend was a youth rally organized by the Diocesan Youth Committee. What the rally really amounted to was a choir get-together. Ten choirs came from as far as 20 miles away. Each choir brought its own flour and dried meat so they were self-contained in terms of food. Ten homes of local Mennonite families received the choirs, giving them a place to cook and providing rooms with reed mats on the floor for sleeping.

The Kirongwe meeting was different from the Ligero one in that only the special guests who came from Shirati in LandRovers were catered for by the local congregation. The diocesan youth officers were in charge of the program which gave things a churchwide flavor. On both Saturday and Sunday a LandRover of missionaries and their guests from the States came up from Shirati, giving a sprinkling of white faces over on the side of the *banda* where the dignitaries and special guests sat.

These get-togethers provide opportunity for young people from far around to meet each other. Dress is important; the best frocks and shirts were saved for the last meeting on Sunday morning. Some of the older girls changed quite often. Several wore three or four outfits on a weekend.

My impression is that a significant portion of the Christian education that young people get in the church is gotten through the songs composed and sung by the choirs. The songs they sing are all original compositions. They pick them up from each other which is one of the values of getting together.

Songs are sung for several years and then forgotten as new ones are composed. I only heard two songs during my three months at Shirati in the summer of 1983 which I had heard eight years earlier when I was a missionary living in that area. Of course at youth rallies any one choir only gets to sing once at a service, a maximum of five appearances on a weekend—Friday night, three services on Saturday, and Sunday morning. So I did not get exposed to a choir's full repertoire.

At Kirongwe I took notes on all the songs sung at the three services I attended, just to see what sort of Christian education is happening. There were of course the Bible stories of Adam and Eve,

Noah, Jonah, and Christmas. Two different songs were about the prodigal son.

One group, an older woman leading a choir made up of her eight teenage sons and daughters, plus a boyfriend, did a little theological overview from Genesis to Revelation detailing the biblical salvation story. Two numbers were a call to be witnesses, five called for repentance, two were on Jesus' death and his saving blood. Fully six numbers were about the day of judgment when the curtain is rung down on history, and four were about the joys of heaven.

The whole congregation sang four numbers from the Mennonite songbook *Tenzi za Rohoni.* These were "Sinners Jesus Will Receive," "At Calvary—Years I Spent in Vanity and Pride," "Come, Ye Sinners, Poor and Wretched," and "I Am Coming to the Cross."

Some of the choir numbers were in Luo and I didn't get translations.

Preaching is a prominent feature of weekend meetings. At these weekend meetings the night rallies are fully given over to the choirs with the exception of a short devotional. But preaching is a prominent feature of the morning and afternoon service. There are either two short sermons of 20 minutes each or one long sermon of 40 minutes. The sermons are presented in two languages, Swahili and the local vernacular. The preacher uses whichever language he is most comfortable with and a translator puts it into the second language. Often a preacher will switch back and forth between two languages, using the one which most succinctly expresses the point he is making, letting the translator cope as best he may.

Before each service the ordained men get together to share with each other where they are in their spiritual life at that point. Often frustrations over travel problems in coming to the conference, or over scheduling at the meetings, are expressed. Someone may share an insight from his morning devotions. Then each pastor is free to say whether or not he has something on his heart which he would like to preach about. Out of this discussion it is decided how many messages there will be, the subject of the messages and the message bearers.

Working at the preaching this way is useful in that the weekend meetings do not become a personal platform for any one preacher. No one coming knows ahead of time who will preach. But there is also a bit of tension because preachers like to preach, especially to large crowds. At Kirongwe there were two African preachers and three missionary preachers, in addition to Bishop Kisare—six men with messages. There was grace among us and we were able to discern together who should speak.

Bishop Kisare preached on Saturday afternoon. A large crowd had gathered from the surrounding *ujamaa* village. He preached on Abraham, directing his message to the youth. I know the Bishop fairly well and knew that his message at Kirongwe was in a large part autobiographical. He kept switching between the past and present tenses.

"Abraham was pitying himself. He has no son. He has no cattle. Before him all is darkness. Sarah, his wife, is barren. He sees that Eliezer of Damascus will inherit his household when he dies. This would be the time for Abraham to say there is no God. This is because people think God must give them everything. But it is not necessary that God enrich you. Some people die before bearing any children. What lack is this to them? None.

"Sometimes I think it would have been better if my mother had never bore me. But she bore me and now I have all this trouble. My wife has no son. I have no cattle. All about me the land is dry.

"God answered Abraham, 'I am your portion.' If God is on my side, and it is my business to see that he is on my side, then I have great wealth. If God is not with me, then I am in great poverty. This is wealth, that God is with you. You put your head to rest at a good place if God is with you.

"When Abraham was a youth he was discouraged and complaining. But God told him, 'My portion to you is great.'

"My dear young people, people tell you that you have been deceived by the Europeans who told you to follow God. But God's salvation was not concocted by the Europeans. God called Abraham long ago when the Europeans were still barbarous savages. God called Abraham out of savagedom. God called Abraham when the Europeans were still practicing witchcraft and divination, when they were savages. Even if others are deceived, don't you be deceived.

"Here I stand a cattle herdsman, a son of Kisare. There are only two of us here today, sons of Kisare who are following God. Most of Kisare's descendants do not know God. Many of Kisare's descendants who began in the way have turned back. And here I preach among those who are Kisare's people. But even if I am the only one to follow God, I have decided to die with my faith.

"There comes a time in everyone's life when he stands alone with his decision. I have experienced much. I have been battered. I am now at a critical place in the battle where I can only go forward on the course I have chosen, entrusting the meaning of my life to God who called me to come out from the traditional ways of my ancestors.

"Going back to Abraham, he died in his faith. First he was pitying himself. God told him how great was his reward. Abraham asked God to open his eyes so he could see. Had his eyes been open, then he would not have complained. God opened his eyes giving him courage to continue on his chosen path.

"Abraham lived to be an old man. All that time the land and the people of the land did not get tired of Abraham. The land gets tired of some people, wishing for them to die. But not Abraham. He became very rich. Why was he so greatly rewarded? Because he chose well in his youth. People who have lived to old age see that he who follows God, his life is good. Why? Because God makes up to him that which he lacks.

"Jacob was a young man running away from home, going to the villages of his mother's brothers, *wajomba*. At night he built a fire so he wouldn't be eaten by wild animals. He slept and saw a ladder with angels climbing and descending. What I want to say is this: Some people think that it is a person's strength of character which enables him to say, 'I have left sin.' This is not true. There is no such person on earth. Rather it is God who guides people to rise above the life of sin.

"Jesus is the ladder. The angels show the worshiper how to climb the ladder, slowly, slowly like a child learning to climb. God is there at the end of the ladder encouraging the travelers saying, 'I am Yahweh and I have made a way for you to come to me.' When Jacob awoke he said, 'God is here. I had put my head at a good place although I did not know it.'

"My dear young people, may my God and your God be with you. Entrust everything to him while you are still young, for his portion is good. Amen."

Busurwa

I was with Bishop Kisare three weekends in a row. Following Ligero, where it rained so much, we went to Busurwa, 16 miles south of Shirati on the lake. We drove cross-country to get there, following cow trails and footpaths.

I liked Busurwa the moment we drove into the place. A big *banda* had been built not far from the lake on a patch of grass next to a cluster of mud-walled, thatched, rectangular, two-room houses. The large space between the houses was clear of weeds and grass, an area carefully swept clean every morning. This layout of *banda* and buildings was situated between two large *kopjes* so one could climb up the rocks and get an eagle's view of the whole thing. It was especially nice for photographing. I would climb the eastern boulder pile in the morning or the western *kopje* in the evening, and thus have perfect lighting with the sun at my back. Always, no matter where I climbed, a score of happy, mischievous boys crowded around. The higher *kopje*, the one to the east, was crowned with a giant fig tree growing out of a crack in the granite, a perfectly delightful place to sit and enjoy the lake breeze. Busurwa is a fertile area supporting a large population. Thatched roofs cluster in *ujamaa* villages here and there across the countryside. I counted five such villages from my perch under the fig tree.

The Busurwa choir was celebrating their winning the trophy shield which designated them the best choir in Bishop Kisare's North Mara Diocese. Usually the Mikondo choir with their two guitars and accordion wins the trophy, but in December 1982, Busurwa made off with the prize. Now at their celebration in July 1983, they put on a big party inviting all their competitors, plus the local Seventh Day Adventist, Pentecostal, and Catholic choirs. Of course their mothers and fathers from the Busurwa Mennonite congregation were there, helping with the work.

The children at these out-of-the-way places are always so excited and curious. We had three tents to put up. All around each effort the children packed in, three and four deep, giving us just room enough to work. There are so many of them in all sizes right down to the one-year-old babies carried around by their three-year-old sisters. I kept wanting to get inside their little viscera, imagining what it all must be like—LandRover, tents, folding cots, sheep and ox being slaughtered, teenage girls bringing wood from the mountain and water from the lake, columns of choir members wheeling into place, drums a-drumming, meat and *ugali* for everyone. . . .

All weekend I never saw an angry scowl or heard a frustrated shout. Everything was organized and everyone was scurrying around having a ball, right down to mother hen clucking importantly about with her ten quarter-grown chicks seeming to say, "See, none of *my* fluff balls were lost to the chicken hawk." The roosters, of course, were a mess, as always, chasing after the hens, even when the hens have chicks—what confusion, chicks all over the place peeping wildly while mom, squawking, is being chased around the granary. It's a bit futile, on the rooster's part, because she never gets caught until her chicks are half grown. Even the black drake was marching around, with his five ducks, trying to stay in the thick of things and being affronted when shooed out of the way.

Early Sunday morning I climbed up the eastern *kopje* to the fig tree to catch a photo before the shadows shortened. Life below was just waking up—cooking fires getting started, teakettles of water for washing up being taken to the various sleeping places, people walking about and asking each other how they had slept. After a bit I saw the Bishop come out of his tent and go over to the LandRover to get something. He couldn't get whatever he wanted because the door was locked and I had the key. So I climbed down and went over to greet him and unlock the vehicle.

Over at both ends of the swept area between the houses, fires were going under great 16-gallon flat-bottomed aluminum kettles, *sufuria*. The one nearest me was attended by three men who were bringing the *sufuria* full of water to boil. It sat on three stones between which one could feed firewood, thus controlling the heat. I joined them. The farther south you get from Shirati, the more Bantu is mixed into the language. I was hearing a lot of Bantu banter at Busurwa. These three men were using it, a throwback to the time before the Nilotic southward migration a couple of centuries ago. I grew up among Bantu people in South Mara so I was able to join in enough of the conversation to give a sense of camaraderie to the proceedings.

After a bit, our water was in a high boil and a woman came over with a three-gallon *sufuria* filled to the brim with a white mixture. "Flour paste," they told me. We men stood back and let her take over. She poured her paste into the water. Almost at once it jelled, too thick for gruel. So she got a bucket of water to thin it down. Now there was too much mixture for the big *sufuria* to hold it all, so she bowled some out into the little *sufuria*. Then she added water to both *sufurias* until she had the consistency she wanted. One of my friends produced a little paper bag full of sugar. He poured about two thirds of it into the gruel while the woman stirred it up. A couple of people helped her set the pot off the fire onto the ground. She added a rock in the fire pit, thus making a smaller triangle so the smaller *sufuria* would fit snugly. She put it on, bringing it also to a boil.

Now it was time for tasting. Since I was by then considered one of the cooks, someone brought me a reclining chair and someone else brought a big china serving bowl full of gruel. I quickly pronounced it first rate, but I noticed a woman taster, standing over on the other side of the big *sufuria*, who was giving her opinion, in Bantu, that the gruel hadn't any sugar at all. Maybe she was referring to what was still in the paper bag. Soon lots of people were tasting here and there. Even a little year-old boy was being helped to taste by his big sister who had a large bowlful. Soon the level in the big sufuria had gone down by two inches so the woman cook called for buckets. Gruel was ladled out and carried off to the various places where choirs were waiting for their breakfast.

I had already had my quart of breakfast but I was summoned

to join the rest of the special guests in the main house. Mama Susana was already there in a pale blue flowered rayon. Every day we were on safari she had a different dress, our bright little grandma. People bring her cloth for presents and she gets the dresses made up, appropriately styled for a bishop's wife. Two great platters full of sliced pawpaw were on the table, for scooping up, with our saucers. Plenty of rich, sweetened milk-tea got my caffeine-starved synapses toned up for the day.

Just then there was a commotion at the door, and two women came in with two great mountains of millet *ugali* and platters of roasted leg of lamb followed by a large bowl of seasoned mutton. Mama, seeing my astonishment, explained that several years earlier a young niece of hers had stayed in her home at Bukiroba while she was taking the domestic science course. The niece, now a married woman, saw this occasion as her opportunity to slaughter a sheep and prepare a special meal for Mama's hospitality. This thanks-feast was wedged between the normal routine of meals at the conference. Of course all of us special guests helped eat it. I don't know what they taught her at the domestic science school, but that woman surely knew how to prepare meats and millet *ugali!*

That Sunday morning the Bishop had a message on his heart, and we four pastors, who were teamed up with him, urged him to preach and to give an invitation. The rest of the time in the service was given to the eight choirs. In his sermon the Bishop spoke on the freedom and healing which a person experiences when he confesses his sin:

"Song is a blessing to our spirits. The singing of the choirs helps to prepare our hearts to receive the gospel message. Your rhythms wakened us from last night's tiredness. Song is a comfort to the discouraged. Maybe a woman here was beaten by her husband last night, and your songs have brought her consolation. Song lifts my spirits when I am tired and depressed. I have always been a singer from my youth. Singing is good. It soothes and comforts, challenges, and stimulates, but song isn't the cure for our problems; the cure is in confession.

"Let us read again our text, Psalm 32.

Blessed is he
    whose transgressions are forgiven,
    whose sins are covered.
Blessed is the man
    whose sin the Lord does not count against him
    and in whose spirit is no deceit.

When I kept silent,
    my bones wasted away

> through my groaning all day long.
> For day and night
>   your hand was heavy upon me;
> my strength was sapped
>   as in the heat of summer.
> Then I acknowledged my sin to you
>   and I did not cover my iniquity.
> I said, 'I will confess
>   my transgressions to the Lord'—
> and you forgave
>   the guilt of my sin....
> You are my hiding place;
>   you will protect me from trouble
>   and surround me with songs of
>   deliverance....

"King David had sinned. He did nothing about his sin. When he kept silent, doing nothing, he wasted away. The sin he carried was slowly destroying him. One day David was wise and brave. He confessed his sin. Only after David confessed his sin did he recover.

"The Ngasaro Choir sang to us of the prodigal son. His life was utterly wasting away. Even his food was only pigs' food. And then he decided to go to his father and confess his sin. This is so simple a thing to do, yet people fear to confess their sin. When the prodigal son came to his father, everything was forgotten that had gone before. The father threw the son's sin far away into forgetfulness and ordered the fattest young bull slain for a welcoming feast. He ordered a garment of great value to be brought and shoes and a ring. All of this grace was released by the son's simple sincere confession.

"The woman taken in adultery and brought before Jesus was to be stoned to death for her sin. Jesus spared her by ordering any man without sin to throw the first stone. Because they all had sin they went away. The woman then confessed her sin before Jesus and he absolved her, setting her free to go home in peace. The only thing Jesus required of her was that she would never return to her sin.

"Naaman, a general in the Syrian army, had leprosy. A Hebrew slave girl in his household quietly told her mistress that, if her master knew, he would go to Israel, to the prophet, and be cured. Naaman got his things together and made the trip. Elisha told him to go to the Jordan River and bathe. Naaman was affronted by this. He considered it an insult to be told to bathe in the Jordan, to be seen by the Hebrews as he cleansed himself in their river. There he was, oozing blood from his sores, refusing to be cured, because he would not expose the nakedness of his condition, preferring to stay hidden with his disease under his robes. When he finally agreed to reveal his condition in a public place, he became well, cleansed of his disease.

"Unconfessed sin destroys you. There was a young man who stole a bicycle. From that day he was so frightened that the police would catch him. His terror of the police was written on his face. You cannot hide the disease of sin in your life. It is seen plainly on your face. On the day that King David was wise and brave and confessed his sin, he could walk about with his face full of joy. Sin deprives us of joy and makes us fear people.

"That knife you stole, that *debe* of cassava you stole that caused that woman to cry so much when she came to the rock where she had left it piled up the evening before, that cow you stole which you used to pay dowry so that now you have married with a stolen cow, the night you banged on your neighbor's door causing him to think the witches were after him so that he was terrified and had no sleep all that night—all these things; then we come to church pretending that everything is all right! But you can not escape from unconfessed sin. It is a cancer eating out your life.

"Sin is a disease destroying relationships and killing people. In years gone by, so many young people have sung in the choirs, but where are they today? They are gone, destroyed by unconfessed sin in their lives. Confession changes everything because then Jesus forgives and cleanses us. People laugh at the simplicity of this medicine for their problems. But this is the only way to get well.

"Confession of our sin is not something we do once and then forget about. It is a way of life practiced by God's people. Even this morning I awoke with fear in my heart, fear of people who would work to undermine my leadership. I confessed this fear to God and told my wife. God set me free.

"Trying to live on this earth is so difficult. Living here is like climbing a great cliff. The rock face is so high and too sheer. We never get far above the base of the cliff. Life keeps knocking us down; we are always slipping back to where we began. But confession of our sin to God frees us and we go right up and over the crag as though on wings! Amen."

Following this message on confession, an invitation was given. About 30 people responded. There were 466 people in attendance that morning.

On the way home late that Sunday afternoon, bushwhacking again over the same trails we had followed Saturday morning, we came on a broad sun-baked meadow filled with crowned cranes, Tanzania's national bird. Their cheeks are snowy white over crimson wattles, the top of the head crowned with a tuft of straw-colored, bristle-like feathers, the forehead velvety black. Their bodies at rest are white, wings etched chestnut and black. I counted 80 of them, more than I had ever seen before in one place.

They were coupling up for the mating season. Crowned cranes do a dance, wings magnificently spread, hopping around in front of each other, somehow thereby getting sorted out who's male and who's female. Slowly the flock is broken up into pairs. When we came on them, it was still pretty early in the mating season and they were just randomly dancing around. They were intent about it and quite oblivious to our big LandRover parked curiously nearby.

Watching the crane dance was, for me, an appropriate concluding experience to the three weekends I had spent on safari with the Kisares attending youth rallies. The LandRover was packed with Africans—men, women, children—and missionaries—two Canadians, one American. It was good to be together, a new community, members of the church, Christ's body on earth.

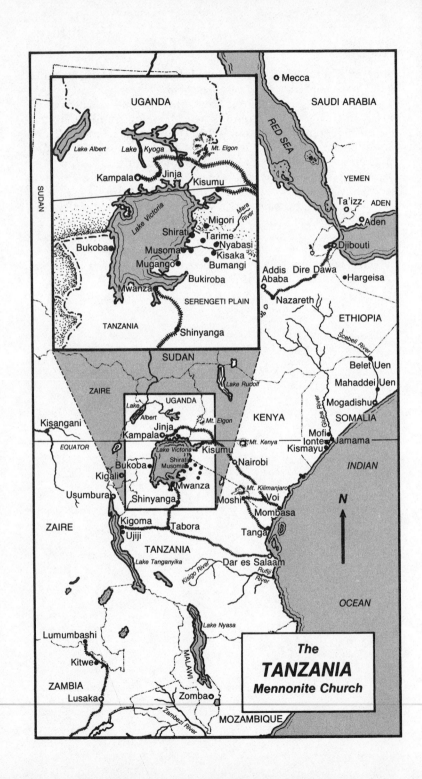

The
TANZANIA
Mennonite Church